A SLIGHT ACHE
and Other Plays

Harold Pinter ENS born in London in 1930. He is
married to Antonia Fraser.

HAROLD PINTER

A Slight Ache
and Other Plays

faber and faber
LONDON · BOSTON

First published in 1961
by Methuen London Ltd
Paperback edition published in 1966
Reprinted with corrections 1968
This edition first published in 1991
by Faber and Faber Limited
3 Queen Square London WCIN 3AU

Printed in England by Clays Ltd, St Ives plc

A CIP record for this book is available from the British Library

ISBN 0-571-16093-X

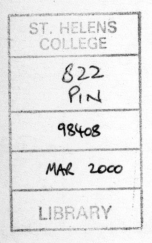

Contents

A Slight Ache

A Slight Ache was first performed on the BBC Third Programme on 9 July 1959, with the following cast:

EDWARD	Maurice Denham
FLORA	Vivien Merchant

Directed by Donald McWhinnie

It was presented by Michael Codron at the Arts Theatre, London, on 18 January 1961, and subsequently at the Criterion Theatre, with the following cast:

EDWARD	Emlyn Williams
FLORA	Alison Leggat
MATCHSELLER	Richard Briers

Directed by Donald McWhinnie

It was produced at the Young Vic in June 1987 with the following cast:

EDWARD	Barry Foster
FLORA	Jill Johnson
MATCHSELLER	Malcolm Ward

Directed by Kevin Billington

A Slight Ache

A country house, with two chairs and a table laid for breakfast
at the centre of the stage. These will later be removed and the
action will be focused on the scullery on the right and the study
on the left, both indicated with a minimum of scenery and
props. A large well kept garden is suggested at the back of the
stage with flower beds, trimmed hedges, etc. The garden gate,
which cannot be seen by the audience, is off right.

FLORA *and* EDWARD *are discovered sitting at the breakfast table.*
EDWARD *is reading the paper.*

FLORA: Have you noticed the honeysuckle this morning?

EDWARD: The what?

FLORA: The honeysuckle.

EDWARD: Honeysuckle? Where?

FLORA: By the back gate, Edward.

EDWARD: Is that honeysuckle? I thought it was . . . convolvulus, or something.

FLORA: But you know it's honeysuckle.

EDWARD: I tell you I thought it was convolvulus.

[*Pause.*]

FLORA: It's in wonderful flower.

EDWARD: I must look.

FLORA: The whole garden's in flower this morning. The
clematis. The convolvulus. Everything. I was out at seven.
I stood by the pool.

EDWARD: Did you say—that the convolvulus was in flower?

FLORA: Yes.

EDWARD: But good God, you just denied there was any.

FLORA: I was talking about the honeysuckle.

EDWARD: About the what?

FLORA [*calmly*]: Edward—you know that shrub outside the toolshed . . .

EDWARD: Yes, yes.

FLORA: That's convolvulus.

EDWARD: That?

FLORA: Yes.

EDWARD: Oh.

[*Pause.*]

I thought it was japonica.

FLORA: Oh, good Lord no.

EDWARD: Pass the teapot, please.

Pause. She pours tea for him.

I don't see why I should be expected to distinguish between these plants. It's not my job.

FLORA: You know perfectly well what grows in your garden.

EDWARD: Quite the contrary. It is clear that I don't.

[*Pause.*]

FLORA [*rising*]: I was up at seven. I stood by the pool. The peace. And everything in flower. The sun was up. You should work in the garden this morning. We could put up the canopy.

EDWARD: The canopy? What for?

FLORA: To shade you from the sun.

EDWARD: Is there a breeze?

FLORA: A light one.

EDWARD: It's very treacherous weather, you know.

[*Pause.*]

FLORA: Do you know what today is?

EDWARD: Saturday.

FLORA: It's the longest day of the year.

EDWARD: Really?

FLORA: It's the height of summer today.

EDWARD: Cover the marmalade.

FLORA: What?

EDWARD: Cover the pot. There's a wasp. [*He puts the paper down on the table.*] Don't move. Keep still. What are you doing?

FLORA: Covering the pot.

EDWARD: Don't move. Leave it. Keep still.

[*Pause.*]

Give me the 'Telegraph'.

FLORA: Don't hit it. It'll bite.

EDWARD: Bite? What do you mean, bite? Keep still.

[*Pause.*]

It's landing.

FLORA: It's going in the pot.

EDWARD: Give me the lid.

FLORA: It's in.

EDWARD: Give me the lid.

FLORA: I'll do it.

EDWARD: Give it to me! Now . . . Slowly . . .

FLORA: What are you doing?

EDWARD: Be quiet. Slowly . . . carefully . . . on . . . the . . . pot! Ha-ha-ha. Very good.

He sits on a chair to the right of the table.

FLORA: Now he's in the marmalade.

EDWARD: Precisely.

Pause. She sits on a chair to the left of the table and reads the 'Telegraph'.

FLORA: Can you hear him?

EDWARD: Hear him?

FLORA: Buzzing.

EDWARD: Nonsense. How can you hear him? It's an earthenware lid.

FLORA: He's becoming frantic.

EDWARD: Rubbish. Take it away from the table.

FLORA: What shall I do with it?

EDWARD: Put it in the sink and drown it.

FLORA: It'll fly out and bite me.

EDWARD: It will not bite you! Wasps don't bite. Anyway, it won't fly out. It's stuck. It'll drown where it is, in the marmalade.

FLORA: What a horrible death.

EDWARD: On the contrary.

[*Pause.*]

FLORA: Have you got something in your eyes?

EDWARD: No. Why do you ask?

FLORA: You keep clenching them, blinking them.

EDWARD: I have a slight ache in them.

FLORA: Oh, dear.

EDWARD: Yes, a slight ache. As if I hadn't slept.

FLORA: Did you sleep, Edward?

EDWARD: Of course I slept. Uninterrupted. As always.

FLORA: And yet you feel tired.

EDWARD: I didn't say I felt tired. I merely said I had a slight ache in my eyes.

FLORA: Why is that, then?

EDWARD: I really don't know.

[*Pause.*]

FLORA: Oh goodness!

EDWARD: What is it?

FLORA: I can see it. It's trying to come out.

EDWARD: How can it?

FLORA: Through the hole. It's trying to crawl out, through the spoon-hole.

EDWARD: Mmmnn, yes. Can't do it, of course. [*Silent pause.*] Well, let's kill it, for goodness' sake.

FLORA: Yes, let's. But how?

EDWARD: Bring it out on the spoon and squash it on a plate.

FLORA: It'll fly away. It'll bite.

EDWARD: If you don't stop saying that word I shall leave this table.

FLORA: But wasps do bite.

EDWARD: They don't bite. They sting. It's snakes . . . that bite.

FLORA: What about horseflies?

[Pause.]

EDWARD [to himself]: Horseflies suck.

[Pause.]

FLORA [tentatively]: If we . . . if we wait long enough, I suppose it'll choke to death. It'll suffocate in the marmalade.

EDWARD [briskly]: You do know I've got work to do this morning, don't you? I can't spend the whole day worrying about a wasp.

FLORA: Well, kill it.

EDWARD: You want to kill it?

FLORA: Yes.

EDWARD: Very well. Pass me the hot water jug.

FLORA: What are you going to do?

EDWARD: Scald it. Give it to me.

She hands him the jug. Pause.

Now . . .

FLORA [whispering]: Do you want me to lift the lid?

EDWARD: No, no, no. I'll pour down the spoon hole. Right . . . down the spoon-hole.

FLORA: Listen!

EDWARD: What?

FLORA: It's buzzing.

EDWARD: Vicious creatures.

[Pause.]

Curious, but I don't remember seeing any wasps at all, all

summer, until now. I'm sure I don't know why. I mean, there must have been wasps.

FLORA: Please.

EDWARD: This couldn't be the first wasp, could it?

FLORA: Please.

EDWARD: The first wasp of summer? No. It's not possible.

FLORA: Edward.

EDWARD: Mmmmmnnn?

FLORA: Kill it.

EDWARD: Ah, yes. Tilt the pot. Tilt. Aah . . . down here . . . right down . . . blinding him . . . that's . . . it.

FLORA: Is it?

EDWARD: Lift the lid. All right, I will. There he is! Dead. What a monster. [*He squashes it on a plate.*]

FLORA: What an awful experience.

EDWARD: What a beautiful day it is. Beautiful. I think I shall work in the garden this morning. Where's that canopy?

FLORA: It's in the shed.

EDWARD: Yes, we must get it out. My goodness, just look at that sky. Not a cloud. Did you say it was the longest day of the year today?

FLORA: Yes.

EDWARD: Ah, it's a good day. I feel it in my bones. In my muscles. I think I'll stretch my legs in a minute. Down to the pool. My God, look at that flowering shrub over there. Clematis. What a wonderful . . . [*He stops suddenly.*]

FLORA: What?

[*Pause.*]

Edward, what is it?

[*Pause.*]

Edward . . .

EDWARD [*thickly*]: He's there.

FLORA: Who?

EDWARD [*low, murmuring*]: Blast and damn it, he's there, he's there at the back gate.

FLORA: Let me see.

She moves over to him to look. Pause.

[*Lightly.*] Oh, it's the matchseller.

EDWARD: He's back again.

FLORA: But he's always there.

EDWARD: Why? What is he doing there?

FLORA: But he's never disturbed you, has he? The man's been standing there for weeks. You've never mentioned it.

EDWARD: What is he doing there?

FLORA: He's selling matches, of course.

EDWARD: It's ridiculous. What's the time?

FLORA: Half past nine.

EDWARD: What in God's name is he doing with a tray full of matches at half past nine in the morning?

FLORA: He arrives at seven o'clock.

EDWARD: Seven o'clock?

FLORA: He's always there at seven.

EDWARD: Yes, but you've never . . . actually seen him arrive?

FLORA: No, I . . .

EDWARD: Well, how do you know he's . . . not been standing there all night?

[*Pause.*]

FLORA: Do you find him interesting, Edward?

EDWARD [*casually*]: Interesting? No. No, I . . . don't find him interesting.

FLORA: He's a very nice old man, really.

EDWARD: You've spoken to him?

FLORA: No. No, I haven't spoken to him. I've nodded.

EDWARD [*pacing up and down*]: For two months he's been standing on that spot, do you realize that? Two months. I haven't been able to step outside the back gate.

FLORA: Why on earth not?

EDWARD [*to himself*]: It used to give me great pleasure, such pleasure, to stroll along through the long grass, out through the back gate, pass into the lane. That pleasure is now denied me. It's my own house, isn't it? It's my own gate.

FLORA: I really can't understand this, Edward.

EDWARD: Damn. And do you know I've never seen him sell one box? Not a box. It's hardly surprising. He's on the wrong road. It's not a road at all. What is it? It's a lane, leading to the monastery. Off everybody's route. Even the monks take a short cut to the village, when they want to go . . . to the village. No one goes up it. Why doesn't he stand on the main road if he wants to sell matches, by the *front* gate? The whole thing's preposterous.

FLORA [*going over to him*]: I don't know why you're getting so excited about it. He's a quiet, harmless old man, going about his business. He's quite harmless.

EDWARD: I didn't say he wasn't harmless. Of course he's harmless. How could he be other than harmless?

Fade out and silence.

FLORA'S *voice, far in the house, drawing nearer.*

FLORA [*off*]: Edward, where are you? Edward? Where are you, Edward?

She appears.

Edward?

Edward, what are you doing in the scullery?

EDWARD [*looking through the scullery window*]: Doing?

FLORA: I've been looking everywhere for you. I put up the canopy ages ago. I came back and you were nowhere to be seen. Have you been out?

EDWARD: No.

FLORA: Where have you been?

EDWARD: Here.

FLORA: I looked in your study. I even went into the attic.

EDWARD [*tonelessly*]: What would I be doing in the attic?

FLORA: I couldn't imagine what had happened to you. Do you know it's twelve o'clock?

EDWARD: Is it?

FLORA: I even went to the bottom of the garden, to see if you were in the toolshed.

EDWARD [*tonelessly*]: What would I be doing in the toolshed?

FLORA: You must have seen me in the garden. You can see through this window.

EDWARD: Only part of the garden.

FLORA: Yes.

EDWARD: Only a corner of the garden. A very small corner.

FLORA: What are you doing in here?

EDWARD: Nothing. I was digging out some notes, that's all.

FLORA: Notes?

EDWARD: For my essay.

FLORA: Which essay?

EDWARD: My essay on space and time.

FLORA: But . . . I've never . . . I don't know that one.

EDWARD: You don't know it?

FLORA: I thought you were writing one about the Belgian Congo.

EDWARD: I've been engaged on the dimensionality and continuity of space . . . and time . . . for years.

FLORA: And the Belgian Congo?

EDWARD [*shortly*]: Never mind about the Belgian Congo.
[*Pause.*]

FLORA: But you don't keep notes in the scullery.

EDWARD: You'd be surprised. You'd be highly surprised.

FLORA: Good Lord, what's that? Is that a bullock let loose? No. It's the matchseller! My goodness, you can see him . . . through the hedge. He looks bigger. Have you been watching him? He looks . . . like a bullock.
[*Pause.*]
Edward?
[*Pause.*]

[*Moving over to him.*] Are you coming outside? I've put up the canopy. You'll miss the best of the day. You can have an hour before lunch.

EDWARD: I've no work to do this morning.

FLORA: What about your essay? You don't intend to stay in the scullery all day, do you?

EDWARD: Get out. Leave me alone.

[*A slight pause.*]

FLORA: Really Edward. You've never spoken to me like that in all your life.

EDWARD: Yes, I have.

FLORA: Oh, Weddie. Beddie-Weddie . . .

EDWARD: Do not call me that!

FLORA: Your eyes are bloodshot.

EDWARD: Damn it.

FLORA: It's too dark in here to peer . . .

EDWARD: Damn.

FLORA: It's so bright outside.

EDWARD: Damn.

FLORA: And it's dark in here.

[*Pause.*]

EDWARD: Christ blast it!

FLORA: You're frightened of him.

EDWARD: I'm not.

FLORA: You're frightened of a poor old man. Why?

EDWARD: I am not!

FLORA: He's a poor, harmless old man.

EDWARD: Aaah my eyes.

FLORA: Let me bathe them.

EDWARD: Keep away.

[*Pause.*]

[*Slowly.*] I want to speak to that man. I want to have a word with him.

[*Pause.*]

It's quite absurd, of course. I really can't tolerate something so . . . absurd, right on my doorstep. I shall not tolerate it. He's sold nothing all morning. No one passed. Yes. A monk passed. A non-smoker. In a loose garment. It's quite obvious he was a non-smoker but still, the man made no effort. He made no effort to clinch a sale, to rid himself of one of his cursed boxes. His one chance, all morning, and he made no effort.

[*Pause.*]

I haven't wasted my time. I've hit, in fact, upon the truth. He's not a matchseller at all. The bastard isn't a matchseller at all. Curious I never realized that before. He's an impostor. I watched him very closely. He made no move towards the monk. As for the monk, the monk made no move towards him. The monk was moving along the lane. He didn't pause, or halt, or in any way alter his step. As for the match-seller—how ridiculous to go on calling him by that title. What a farce. No, there is something very false about that man. I intend to get to the bottom of it. I'll soon get rid of him He can go and ply his trade somewhere else. Instead of standing like a bullock . . . a bullock, outside my back gate.

FLORA: But if he isn't a matchseller, what is his trade?

EDWARD: We'll soon find out.

FLORA: You're going out to speak to him?

EDWARD: Certainly not! Go out to *him*? Certainly . . . not. I'll invite him in here. Into my study. Then we'll . . . get to the bottom of it.

FLORA: Why don't you call the police and have him removed?

He laughs. Pause.

Why don't you call the police, Edward? You could say he was a public nuisance. Although I . . . I can't say I find him a nuisance.

EDWARD: Call him in.

FLORA: Me?

EDWARD: Go out and call him in.

FLORA: Are you serious?

[*Pause.*]

Edward, I could call the police. Or even the vicar.

EDWARD: Go and get him.

She goes out. Silence.

EDWARD *waits.*

FLORA [*in the garden*]: Good morning.

[*Pause.*]

We haven't met. I live in this house here. My husband and I.

[*Pause.*]

I wonder if you could . . . would you care for a cup of tea?

[*Pause.*]

Or a glass of lemon? It must be so dry, standing here.

[*Pause.*]

Would you like to come inside for a little while? It's much cooler. There's something we'd very much like to . . . tell you, that will benefit you. Could you spare a few moments? We won't keep you long.

[*Pause.*]

Might I buy your tray of matches, do you think? We've run out, completely, and we always keep a very large stock. It happens that way, doesn't it? Well, we can discuss it inside. Do come. This way. Ah now, do come. Our house is full of curios, you know. My husband's been rather a collector. We have goose for lunch. Do you care for goose?

She moves to the gate.

Come and have lunch with us. This way. That's . . . right. May I take your arm? There's a good deal of *nettle* inside the gate. [*The* MATCHSELLER *appears.*] Here. This way. Mind now. Isn't it beautiful weather? It's the longest day of the year today.

[*Pause.*]

That's honeysuckle. And that's convolvulus. There's clematis. And do you see that plant by the conservatory? That's japonica.

Silence. She enters the study.

FLORA: He's here.

EDWARD: I know.

FLORA: He's in the hall.

EDWARD: I know he's here. I can smell him.

FLORA: Smell him?

EDWARD: I smelt him when he came under my window. Can't you smell the house now?

FLORA: What are you going to do with him, Edward? You won't be rough with him in any way? He's very old. I'm not sure if he can hear, or even see. And he's wearing the oldest—

EDWARD: I don't want to know what he's wearing.

FLORA: But you'll see for yourself in a minute, if you speak to him.

EDWARD: I shall.

[*Slight pause.*]

FLORA: He's an old man. You won't ... be rough with him?

EDWARD: If he's so old, why doesn't he seek shelter ... from the storm?

FLORA: But there's no storm. It's summer, the longest day ...

EDWARD: There was a storm, last week. A summer storm. He stood without moving, while it raged about him.

FLORA: When was this?

EDWARD: He remained quite still, while it thundered all about him.

[*Pause.*]

FLORA: Edward ... are you sure it's wise to bother about all this?

EDWARD: Tell him to come in.

FLORA: I . . .
EDWARD: Now.

She goes and collects the MATCHSELLER.

FLORA: Hullo. Would you like to go in? I won't be long.
Up these stairs here.
[*Pause.*]
You can have some sherry before lunch.
[*Pause.*]
Shall I take your tray? No. Very well, take it with you.
Just . . . up those stairs. The door at the . . .
[*She watches him move.*]
the door . . .
[*Pause.*]
the door at the top. I'll join you . . . later. [*She goes out.*]

The MATCHSELLER *stands on the threshold of the study.*

EDWARD [*cheerfully*]: Here I am. Where are you?
[*Pause.*]
Don't stand out there, old chap. Come into my study.
[*He rises.*] Come in.

The MATCHSELLER *enters.*

That's right. Mind how you go. That's . . . it. Now.
make yourself comfortable. Thought you might like some
refreshment, on a day like this. Sit down, old man. What
will you have? Sherry? Or what about a double scotch? Eh?
[*Pause.*]
I entertain the villagers annually, as a matter of fact. I'm
not the squire, but they look upon me with some regard.
Don't believe we've got a squire here any more, actually.
Don't know what became of him. Nice old man he was.
Great chess-player, as I remember. Three daughters. The
pride of the county. Flaming red hair. Alice was the eldest.
Sit yourself down, old chap. Eunice I think was number

two. The youngest one was the best of the bunch. Sally.
No, no, wait a minute, no, it wasn't Sally, it was . . .
Fanny. Fanny. A flower. You must be a stranger here.
Unless you lived here once, went on a long voyage and
have lately returned. Do you know the district?
[*Pause.*]
Now, now, you mustn't . . . stand about like that. Take
a seat. Which one would you prefer? We have a great
variety, as you see. Can't stand uniformity. Like different
seats, different backs. Often when I'm working, you know,
I draw up one chair, scribble a few lines, put it by, draw
up another, sit back, ponder, put it by . . . [*absently*]
. . . sit back . . . put it by . . .
[*Pause.*]
I write theological and philosophical essays . . .
[*Pause.*]
Now and again I jot down a few observations on certain
tropical phenomena—not from the same standpoint, of
course. [*Silent pause.*] Yes. Africa, now. Africa's always
been my happy hunting ground. Fascinating country. Do
you know it? I get the impression that you've . . . been
around a bit. Do you by any chance know the Membunza
Mountains? Great range south of Katambaloo. French
Equatorial Africa, if my memory serves me right. Most
extraordinary diversity of flora and fauna. Especially fauna.
I understand in the Gobi Desert you can come across
some very strange sights. Never been there myself. Studied
the maps though. Fascinating things, maps.
[*Pause.*]
Do you live in the village? I don't often go down, of course.
Or are you passing through? On your way to another part
of the country? Well, I can tell you, in my opinion you
won't find many prettier parts than here. We win the first
prize regularly, you know, the best kept village in the area.
Sit down.

[*Pause.*]

I say, can you hear me?

[*Pause.*]

I said, I say, can you hear me?

[*Pause.*]

You possess most extraordinary repose, for a man of your age, don't you? Well, perhaps that's not quite the right word . . . repose. Do you find it chilly in here? I'm sure it's chillier in here than out. I haven't been out yet, today, though I shall probably spend the whole afternoon working, in the garden, under my canopy, at my table, by the pool. [*Pause.*]

Oh, I understand you met my *wife*? Charming woman, don't you think? Plenty of grit there, too. Stood by me through thick and thin, that woman. In season and out of season. Fine figure of a woman she was, too, in her youth. Wonderful carriage, flaming red hair. [*He stops abruptly.*]

[*Pause.*]

Yes, I . . . I was in much the same position myself then as you are now, you understand. Struggling to make my way in the world. I was in commerce too. [*With a chuckle.*] Oh, yes, I know what it's like—the weather, the rain, beaten from pillar to post, up hill and down dale . . . the rewards were few . . . winters in hovels . . . up till all hours working at your thesis . . . yes, I've done it all. Let me advise you. Get a good woman to stick by you. Never mind what the world says. Keep at it. Keep your shoulder to the wheel. It'll pay dividends.

Pause.

[*With a laugh.*] You must excuse my chatting away like this. We have few visitors this time of the year. All our friends summer abroad. I'm a home bird myself. Wouldn't mind taking a trip to Asia Minor, mind you, or to certain lower regions of the Congo, but Europe? Out of the question. Much too noisy. I'm sure you agree. Now look, what will you have to drink? A glass of ale? Curaçao Fockink Orange? Ginger beer? Tia Maria? A Wachenheimer Fuchsmantel Reisling Beeren Auslese? Gin and it? Chateauneuf-du-Pape? A little Asti Spumante? Or what do you say to a straightforward Piesporter Goldtropfschen Feine Auslese (Reichsgraf von Kesselstaff)? Any preference?

[*Pause.*]

You look a trifle warm. Why don't you take off your balaclava? I'd find that a little itchy myself. But then I've always been one for freedom of movement. Even in the depth of winter I wear next to nothing.

[*Pause.*]

I say, can I ask you a personal question? I don't want to seem inquisitive but aren't you rather on the wrong road for matchselling? Not terribly busy, is it? Of course you may not care for petrol fumes or the noise of traffic. I can quite understand that.

[*Pause.*]

Do forgive me peering but is that a glass eye you're wearing?

[*Pause.*]

Do take off your balaclava, there's a good chap, put your tray down and take your ease, as they say in this part of the world. [*He moves towards him.*] I must say you keep quite a good stock, don't you? Tell me, between ourselves, are those boxes full, or are there just a few half-empty ones among them? Oh yes, I used to be in commerce. Well now, before the good lady sounds the gong for petit déjeuner will you join me in an apéritif? I recommend a glass of cider. Now . . . just a minute . . . I know I've got some—Look out! Mind your tray!

The tray falls, and the matchboxes.

Good God, what . . . ?

[*Pause.*]
You've dropped your tray.

Pause. He picks the matchboxes up.

[*Grunts.*] Eh, these boxes are all wet. You've no right to
sell wet matches, you know. Uuuuugggh. This feels suspiciously like fungus. You won't get very far in this trade
if you don't take care of your goods. [*Grunts, rising.*] Well,
here you are.
[*Pause.*]
Here's your tray.

He puts the tray into the MATCHSELLER'S *hands, and sits.
Pause.*

Now listen, let me be quite frank with you, shall I? I
really cannot understand why you don't sit down. There
are four chairs at your disposal. Not to mention the hassock.
I can't possibly talk to you unless you're settled. Then and
only then can I speak to you. Do you follow me? You're
not being terribly helpful. [*Slight pause.*] You're sweating.
The sweat's pouring out of you. Take off that balaclava.
[*Pause.*]
Go into the corner then. Into the corner. Go on. Get into
the shade of the corner. Back. Backward.
[*Pause.*]
Get back!
[*Pause.*]
Ah, you understand me. Forgive me for saying so, but I
had decided that you had the comprehension of a bullock.
I was mistaken. You understand me perfectly well. That's
right. A little more. A little to the right. Aaah. Now you're
there. In shade, in shadow. Good-o. Now I can get down
to brass tacks. Can't I?
[*Pause.*]

No doubt you're wondering why I invited you into this house? You may think I was alarmed by the look of you. You would be quite mistaken. I was not alarmed by the look of you. I did not find you at all alarming. No, no. Nothing outside this room has ever alarmed me. You disgusted me, quite forcibly, if you want to know the truth. [*Pause.*]
Why did you disgust me to that extent? That seems to be a pertinent question. You're no more disgusting than Fanny, the squire's daughter, after all. In appearance you differ but not in essence. There's the same . . .
[*Pause.*]
The same . . .
[*Pause.*]
[*In a low voice.*] I want to ask you a question. Why do you stand outside my back gate, from dawn till dusk, why do you pretend to sell matches, why . . . ? What is it, damn you. You're shivering. You're sagging. Come here, come here . . . mind your tray! [EDWARD *rises and moves behind a chair.*] Come, quick quick. There. Sit here. Sit . . . sit in this.

The MATCHSELLER *stumbles and sits. Pause.*

Aaaah! You're sat. At last. What a relief. You must be tired. [*Slight pause.*] Chair comfortable? I bought it in a sale. I bought all the furniture in this house in a sale. The same sale. When I was a young man. You too, perhaps. You too, perhaps.
[*Pause.*]
At the same time, perhaps!
[*Pause.*]
[*Muttering.*] I must get some air. I must get a breath of air.

He goes to the door.

Flora!

FLORA: Yes?

EDWARD [*with great weariness*]: Take me into the garden.

Silence. They move from the study door to a chair under a canopy.

FLORA: Come under the canopy.

EDWARD: Ah. [*He sits.*]

[*Pause.*]

The peace. The peace out here.

FLORA: Look at our trees.

EDWARD: Yes.

FLORA: Our own trees. Can you hear the birds?

EDWARD: No, I can't hear them.

FLORA: But they're singing, high up, and flapping.

EDWARD: Good. Let them flap.

FLORA: Shall I bring your lunch out here? You can have it in peace, and a quiet drink, under your canopy.

[*Pause.*]

How are you getting on with your old man?

EDWARD: What do you mean?

FLORA: What's happening? How are you getting on with him?

EDWARD: Very well. We get on remarkably well. He's a little . . . reticent. Somewhat withdrawn. It's understandable. I should be the same, perhaps, in his place. Though, of course, I could not possibly find myself in his place.

FLORA: Have you found out anything about him?

EDWARD: A little. A little. He's had various trades, that's certain. His place of residence is unsure. He's . . . he's not a drinking man. As yet, I haven't discovered the reason for his arrival here. I shall in due course . . . by nightfall.

FLORA: Is it necessary?

EDWARD: Necessary?

FLORA [*quickly sitting on the right arm of the chair*]: I could show him out now, it wouldn't matter. You've seen him, he's harmless, unfortunate . . . old, that's all. Edward—

listen—he's not here through any . . . design, or anything,
I know it. I mean, he might just as well stand outside our
back gate as anywhere else. He'll move on. I can . . . make
him. I promise you. There's no point in upsetting yourself
like this. He's an old man, weak in the head . . . that's all.
[*Pause.*]

EDWARD: You're deluded.

FLORA: Edward—

EDWARD [*rising*]: You're deluded. And stop calling me Edward.

FLORA: You're not still frightened of him?

EDWARD: Frightened of him? Of *him*? Have you *seen* him?
[*Pause.*]
He's like jelly. A great bullockfat of jelly.. He can't see
straight. I think as a matter of fact he wears a glass eye.
He's almost stone deaf . . . almost . . . not quite. He's
very nearly dead on his feet. Why should he frighten me?
No, you're a woman, you know nothing. [*Slight pause.*]
But he possesses other faculties. Cunning. The man's an
imposter and he knows I know it.

FLORA: I'll tell you what. Look. Let me speak to him. I'll
speak to him.

EDWARD [*quietly*]: And I know he knows I know it.

FLORA: I'll find out all about him, Edward. I promise you I
will.

EDWARD: And he knows I know.

FLORA: Edward! Listen to me! I can find out all about him,
I promise you. I shall go and have a word with him now.
I shall . . . get to the bottom of it.

EDWARD: You? It's laughable.

FLORA: You'll see—he won't bargain for me. I'll surprise
him. He'll . . . he'll admit everything.

EDWARD [*softly*]: He'll admit everything, will he?

FLORA: You wait and see, you just—

EDWARD [*hissing*]: What are you plotting?

FLORA: I know exactly what I shall—

EDWARD: What are you plotting?

He seizes her arms.

FLORA: Edward, you're hurting me!
[*Pause.*]
[*With dignity.*] I shall wave from the window when I'm ready. Then you can come up. I shall get to the truth of it, I assure you. You're much too heavy-handed, in every way. You should trust your wife more, Edward. You should trust her judgment, and have a greater insight into her capabilities. A woman . . . a woman will often succeed, you know, where a man must invariably fail.

Silence. She goes into the study.

Do you mind if I come in?

The door closes.

Are you comfortable?
[*Pause.*]
Oh, the sun's shining directly on you. Wouldn't you rather sit in the shade?

She sits down.

It's the longest day of the year today, did you know that? Actually the year has flown. I can remember Christmas and that dreadful frost. And the floods! I hope you weren't here in the floods. We were out of danger up here, of course, but in the valleys whole families I remember drifted away on the current. The country was a lake. Everything stopped. We lived on our own preserves, drank elderberry wine, studied other cultures.
[*Pause.*]
Do you know, I've got a feeling I've seen you before, somewhere. Long before the flood. You were much younger. Yes, I'm really sure of it. Between ourselves, were you ever

a poacher? I had an encounter with a poacher once. It was
a ghastly rape, the brute. High up on a hillside cattle track.
Early spring. I was out riding on my pony. And there on the
verge a man lay—ostensibly injured, lying on his front, I
remember, possibly the victim of a murderous assault, how
was I to know? I dismounted, I went to him, he rose, I
fell, my pony took off, down to the valley. I saw the sky
through the trees, blue. Up to my ears in mud. It was a
desperate battle.

[*Pause.*]

I lost.

[*Pause.*]

Of course, life was perilous in those days. It was my first
canter unchaperoned.

[*Pause.*]

Years later, when I was a Justice of the Peace for the county,
I had him in front of the bench. He was there for poaching.
That's how I know he was a poacher. The evidence though
was sparse, inadmissible, I acquitted him, letting him off
with a caution. He'd grown a red beard, I remember. Yes.
A bit of a stinker.

[*Pause.*]

I say, you are perspiring, aren't you? Shall I mop your
brow? With my chiffon? Is it the heat? Or the closeness?
Or confined space? Or . . .? [*She goes over to him.*]
Actually, the day is cooling. It'll soon be dusk. Perhaps it
is dusk. May I? You don't mind?

[*Pause. She mops his brow.*]

Ah, there, that's better. And your cheeks. It is a woman's
job, isn't it? And I'm the only woman on hand. There.

Pause. She leans on the arm of chair.

[*Intimately.*] Tell me, have you a woman? Do you like
women? Do you ever . . . think about women?

[*Pause.*]

Have you ever . . . stopped a woman?

[*Pause.*]

I'm sure you must have been quite attractive once. [*She sits.*] Not any more, of course. You've got a vile smell. Vile. Quite repellent, in fact.

[*Pause.*]

Sex, I suppose, means nothing to you. Does it ever occur to you that sex is a very vital experience for other people? Really, I think you'd amuse me if you weren't so hideous. You're probably quite amusing in your own way. [*Seductively.*] Tell me all about love. Speak to me of love.

[*Pause.*]

God knows what you're saying at this very moment. It's quite disgusting. Do you know when I was a girl I loved . . . I loved . . . I simply adored . . . what *have* you got on, for goodness sake? A jersey? It's clogged. Have you been rolling in mud? [*Slight pause.*] You haven't been rolling in mud, have you? [*She rises and goes over to him.*] And what have you got under your jersey? Let's see. [*Slight pause.*] I'm not tickling you, am I? No. Good . . . Lord, is this a vest? That's quite original. Quite original. [*She sits on the arm of his chair.*] Hmmnn, you're a solid old boy, I must say. Not at all like a jelly. All you need is a bath. A lovely lathery bath. And a good scrub. A lovely lathery scrub. [*Pause.*] Don't you? It will be a pleasure. [*She throws her arms round him.*] I'm going to keep you. I'm going to keep you, you dreadful chap, and call you Barnabas. Isn't it dark, Barnabas? Your eyes, your eyes, your great big eyes.

Pause.

My husband would never have guessed your name. Never. [*She kneels at his feet. Whispering.*] It's me you were waiting for, wasn't it? You've been standing waiting for me. You've seen me in the woods, picking daisies, in my apron, my pretty daisy apron, and you came and stood, poor creature, at my gate, till death us do part. Poor Barnabas. I'm going to put you to bed. I'm going to put you to bed and watch over you. But first you must have a good whacking great bath. And I'll buy you pretty little things that will suit you. And little toys to play with. On your deathbed. Why shouldn't you die happy?

A shout from the hall.

EDWARD: Well?
   [*Footsteps upstage.*]
   Well?
FLORA: Don't come in.
EDWARD: Well?
FLORA: He's dying.
EDWARD: Dying? He's not dying.
FLORA: I tell you, he's very ill.
EDWARD: He's not dying! Nowhere near. He'll see you cremated.
FLORA: The man is desperately ill!
EDWARD: Ill? You lying slut. Get back to your trough!
FLORA: Edward . . .
EDWARD [*violently*]: To your trough!

She goes out. Pause.

[*Coolly.*] Good evening to you. Why are you sitting in the gloom? Oh, you've begun to disrobe. Too warm? Let's open these windows, then, what?

He opens the windows.

Pull the blinds.

He pulls the blinds.

And close . . . the curtains . . . again.

He closes the curtains.

Ah. Air will enter through the side chinks. Of the blinds.
And filter through the curtains. I hope. Don't want to
suffocate, do we?

[*Pause.*]

More comfortable? Yes. You look different in darkness.
Take off all your togs, if you like. Make yourself at home.
Strip to your buff. Do as you would in your own house.

[*Pause.*]

Did you say something?

[*Pause.*]

Did you say something?

[*Pause.*]

Anything? Well then, tell me about your boyhood. Mmnn?

[*Pause.*]

What did you do with it? Run? Swim? Kick the ball?
You kicked the ball? What position? Left back? Goalie?
First reserve?

[*Pause.*]

I used to play myself. Country house matches, mostly.
Kept wicket and batted number seven.

[*Pause.*]

Kept wicket and batted number seven. Man called—
Cavendish, I think had something of your style. Bowled
left arm over the wicket, always kept his cap on, quite a
dab hand at solo whist, preferred a good round of prop and
cop to anything else.

[*Pause.*]

On wet days when the field was swamped.

[*Pause.*]

Perhaps you don't play cricket.

[*Pause.*]

Perhaps you never met Cavendish and never played cricket.
You look less and less like a cricketer the more I see of you.
Where did you live in those days? God damn it, I'm en-
titled to know something about you! You're in my blasted

house, on my territory, drinking my wine, eating my duck!
Now you've had your fill you sit like a hump, a mouldering
heap. In my room. My den. I can rem . . . [*He stops
abruptly.*]

[*Pause.*]

You find that funny? Are you grinning?

[*Pause.*]

[*In disgust.*] Good Christ, is that a grin on your face?
[*Further disgust.*] It's lopsided. It's all—down on one side.
You're grinning. It amuses you, does it? When I tell you
how well I remember this room, how well I remember
this den. [*Muttering.*] Ha. Yesterday now, it was clear,
clearly defined, so clearly.

[*Pause.*]

The garden, too, was sharp, lucid, in the rain, in the sun.

[*Pause.*]

My den, too, was sharp, arranged for my purpose . . .
quite satisfactory.

[*Pause.*]

The house too, was polished, all the banisters were polished,
and the stair rods, and the curtain rods.

[*Pause.*]

My desk was polished, and my cabinet.

[*Pause.*]

I was polished. [*Nostalgic.*] I could stand on the hill and
look through my telescope at the sea. And follow the path
of the three-masted schooner, feeling fit, well aware of my
sinews, their suppleness, my arms lifted holding the
telescope, steady, easily, no trembling, my aim was perfect,
I could pour hot water down the spoon-hole, yes, easily, no
difficulty, my grasp firm, my command established, my
life was accounted for, I was ready for my excursions to the
cliff, down the path to the back gate, through the long
grass, no need to watch for the nettles, my progress was
fluent, after my long struggling against all kinds of usurpers,

disreputables, lists, literally lists of people anxious to do me down, and my reputation down, my command was established, all summer I would breakfast, survey my landscape, take my telescope, examine the overhanging of my hedges, pursue the narrow lane past the monastery, climb the hill, adjust the lens [*he mimes a telescope*], watch the progress of the three-masted schooner, my progress was as sure, as fluent . . .

Pause. He drops his arms.

Yes, yes, you're quite right, it is funny.
[*Pause.*]
Laugh your bloody head off! Go on. Don't mind me. No need to be polite.
[*Pause.*]
That's right.
[*Pause.*]
You're quite right, it is funny. I'll laugh with you!

He laughs.

Ha-ha-ha! Yes! You're laughing with me, I'm laughing with you, we're laughing together!

He laughs and stops.

[*Brightly.*] Why did I invite you into this room? That's your next question, isn't it? Bound to be.
[*Pause.*]
Well, why not, you might say? My oldest acquaintance. My nearest and dearest. My kith and kin. But surely correspondence would have been as satisfactory . . . more satisfactory? We could have exchanged postcards, couldn't we? What? Views, couldn't we? Of sea and land, city and village, town and country, autumn and winter . . . clocktowers . . . museums . . . citadels . . . bridges . . . rivers . . .

[*Pause.*]

Seeing you stand, at the back gate, such close proximity, was not at all the same thing.

[*Pause.*]

What are you doing? You're taking off your balaclava . . . you've decided not to. No, very well then, all things considered, did I then invite you into this room with express intention of asking you to take off your balaclava, in order to determine your resemblance to—some other person? The answer is no, certainly not, I did not, for when I first saw you you wore no balaclava. No headcovering of any kind, in fact. You looked quite different without a head—I mean without a hat—I mean without a headcovering, of any kind. In fact every time I have seen you you have looked quite different to the time before.

[*Pause.*]

Even now you look different. Very different.

[*Pause.*]

Admitted that sometimes I viewed you through dark glasses, yes, and sometimes through light glasses, and on other occasions bare eyed, and on other occasions through the bars of the scullery window, or from the roof, the roof, yes in driving snow, or from the bottom of the drive in thick fog, or from the roof again in blinding sun, so blinding, so hot, that I had to skip and jump and bounce in order to remain in one place. Ah, that's good for a guffaw, is it? That's good for a belly laugh? Go on, then. Let it out. Let yourself go, for God's . . . [*He catches his breath.*] You're crying . . .

[*Pause.*]

[*Moved.*] You haven't been laughing. You're crying.

[*Pause.*]

You're weeping. You're shaking with grief. For me. I can't believe it. For my plight. I've been wrong.

[*Pause.*]

[*Briskly.*] Come, come, stop it. Be a man. Blow your nose for goodness sake. Pull yourself together.

He sneezes.

Ah.

He rises. Sneeze.

Ah. Fever. Excuse me.

He blows his nose.

I've caught a cold. A germ. In my eyes. It was this morning. In my eyes. My eyes.

Pause. He falls to the floor.

Not that I had any difficulty in seeing you, no, no, it was not so much my sight, my sight is excellent—in winter I run about with nothing on but a pair of polo shorts—no, it was not so much any deficiency in my sight as the airs between me and my object—don't weep—the change of air, the currents obtaining in the space between me and my object, the shades they make, the shapes they take, the quivering, the eternal quivering—please stop crying—nothing to do with heat-haze. Sometimes, of course, I would take shelter, shelter to compose myself. Yes, I would seek a tree, a cranny of bushes, erect my canopy and so make shelter. And rest. [*Low murmur.*] And then I no longer heard the wind or saw the sun. Nothing entered, nothing left my nook. I lay on my side in my polo shorts, my fingers lightly in contact with the blades of grass, the earthflowers, the petals of the earth-flowers flaking, lying on my palm, the underside of all the great foliage dark, above me, but it is only afterwards I say the foliage was dark, the petals flaking, then I said nothing, I remarked nothing, things happened upon me, then in my times of shelter, the shades, the petals, carried themselves, carried their bodies upon me, and nothing entered my nook, nothing left it.

[*Pause.*]
But then, the time came. I saw the wind. I saw the wind, swirling, and the dust at my back gate, lifting, and the long grass, scything together . . . [*Slowly, in horror.*] You *are* laughing. You're laughing. Your face. Your body. [*Overwhelming nausea and horror.*] Rocking . . . gasping . . . rocking . . . shaking . . . rocking . . . heaving . . . rocking . . . You're laughing at me! Aaaaahhhh!

The MATCHSELLER *rises. Silence.*

You look younger. You look extraordinarily . . . youthful.
[*Pause.*]
You want to examine the garden? It must be very bright, in the moonlight. [*Becoming weaker.*] I would like to join you . . . explain . . . show you . . . the garden . . . explain . . . The plants . . . where I run . . . my track . . . in training . . . I was number one sprinter at Howells . . . when a stripling . . . no more than a stripling . . . licked . . . men twice my strength . . . when a stripling . . . like yourself.
[*Pause.*]
[*Flatly.*] The pool must be glistening. In the moonlight. And the lawn. I remember it well. The cliff. The sea. The three-masted schooner.
[*Pause.*]
[*With great, final effort—a whisper.*] Who are you?
FLORA [*off*]: Barnabas?
[*Pause.*]

She enters.

Ah, Barnabas. Everything is ready.
[*Pause.*]
I want to show you my garden, your garden. You must see my japonica, .my convolvulus . . . my honeysuckle, my clematis.

[*Pause.*]

The summer is coming. I've put up your canopy for you. You can lunch in the garden, by the pool. I've polished the whole house for you.

[*Pause.*]

Take my hand.

Pause. The MATCHSELLER *goes over to her.*

Yes. Oh, wait a moment.

[*Pause.*]

Edward. Here is your tray.

She crosses to EDWARD *with the tray of matches, and puts it in his hands. Then she and the* MATCHSELLER *start to go out as the curtain falls slowly.*

A Night Out

A Night Out was first performed on the B.B.C. Third Programme on 1 March 1960, with the following cast:

ALBERT STOKES	Barry Foster
MRS. STOKES, *his mother*	Mary O'Farrell
SEELEY	Harold Pinter
KEDGE	John Rye
BARMAN AT THE COFFEE STALL	Walter Hall
OLD MAN	Norman Wynne
MR. KING	David Bird
MR. RYAN	Norman Wynne
GIDNEY	Nicholas Selby
JOYCE	Jane Jordan Rogers
EILEEN	Auriol Smith
BETTY	Margaret Hotine
HORNE	Hugh Dickson
BARROW	David Spenser
THE GIRL	Vivien Merchant

Produced by Donald McWhinnie

The play was televised by A.B.C. Armchair Theatre on 24 April 1960, with the following cast:

ALBERT STOKES	Tom Bell
MRS. STOKES, *his mother*	Madge Ryan
SEELEY	Harold Pinter
KEDGE	Philip Locke
BARMAN AT THE COFFEE STALL	Edmond Bennett
OLD MAN	Gordon Phillott
MR. KING	Arthur Lowe
MR. RYAN	Edward Malin
GIDNEY	Stanley Meadows
JOYCE	José Read
EILEEN	Maria Lennard
BETTY	Mary Duddy
HORNE	Stanley Segal
BARROW	Walter Hall
THE GIRL	Vivien Merchant

Produced by Philip Saville

Act One

SCENE ONE

The kitchen of MRS. STOKES' *small house in the south of London.*
Clean and tidy.

ALBERT, *a young man of twenty-eight, is standing in his shirt*
and trousers, combing his hair in the kitchen mirror over the
mantelpiece. A woman's voice calls his name from upstairs.
He ignores it, picks up a brush from the mantelpiece and brushes
his hair. The voice calls again. He slips the comb in his pocket,
bends down, reaches under the sink and takes out a shoe
duster. He begins to polish his shoes. MRS. STOKES *descends*
the stairs, passes through the hall and enters the kitchen.

MOTHER: Albert, I've been calling you. [*She watches him.*]
    What are you doing?
ALBERT: Nothing.
MOTHER: Didn't you hear me call you, Albert? I've been
    calling you from upstairs.
ALBERT: You seen my tie?
MOTHER: Oh, I say, I'll have to put the flag out.
ALBERT: What do you mean?
MOTHER: Cleaning your shoes, Albert? I'll have to put the
    flag out, won't I?

    ALBERT *puts the brush back under the sink and begins to search*
    the sideboard and cupboard.

    What are you looking for?
ALBERT: My tie. The striped one, the blue one.
MOTHER: The bulb's gone in Grandma's room.

ALBERT: Has it?

MOTHER: That's what I was calling you about. I went in and switched on the light and the bulb had gone.

She watches him open the kitchen cabinet and look into it.

Aren't those your best trousers, Albert? What have you put on your best trousers for?

ALBERT: Look, Mum, where's my tie? The blue one, the blue tie, where is it? You know the one I mean, the blue striped one, I gave it to you this morning.

MOTHER: What do you want your tie for?

ALBERT: I want to put it on. I asked you to press it for me this morning. I gave it to you this morning before I went to work, didn't I?

She goes to the gas stove, examines the vegetables, opens the oven and looks into it.

MOTHER [*gently*]: Well, your dinner'll be ready soon. You can look for it afterwards. Lay the table, there's a good boy.

ALBERT: Why should I look for it afterwards? You know where it is now.

MOTHER: You've got five minutes. Go down to the cellar, Albert, get a bulb and put it in Grandma's room, go on.

ALBERT [*irritably*]: I don't know why you keep calling that room Grandma's room, she's been dead ten years.

MOTHER: Albert!

ALBERT: I mean, it's just a junk room, that's all it is.

MOTHER: Albert, that's no way to speak about your Grandma, you know that as well as I do.

ALBERT: I'm not saying a word against Grandma—

MOTHER: You'll upset me in a minute, you go on like that.

ALBERT: I'm not going on about anything.

MOTHER: Yes, you are. Now why don't you go and put a bulb in Grandma's room and by the time you come down I'll have your dinner on the table.

ALBERT: I can't go down to the cellar, I've got my best trousers on, I've got a white shirt on.

MOTHER: You're dressing up tonight, aren't you? Dressing up, cleaning your shoes, anyone would think you were going to the Ritz.

ALBERT: I'm not going to the Ritz.

MOTHER [*suspiciously*]: What do you mean, you're not going to the Ritz?

ALBERT: What do you mean?

MOTHER: The way you said you're not going to the Ritz, it sounded like you were going somewhere else.

ALBERT [*wearily*]: I am.

MOTHER [*shocked surprise*]: You're going out?

ALBERT: You know I'm going out. I told you I was going out. I told you last week. I told you this morning. Look, where's my tie? I've got to have my tie. I'm late already. Come on, Mum, where'd you put it?

MOTHER: What about your dinner?

ALBERT [*searching*]: Look . . . I told you . . . I haven't got the . . . wait a minute . . . ah, here it is.

MOTHER: You can't wear that tie. I haven't pressed it.

ALBERT: You have. Look at it. Of course you have. It's beautifully pressed. It's fine.

He ties the tie.

MOTHER: Where are you going?

ALBERT: Mum, I've told you, honestly, three times. Honestly, I've told you three times I had to go out tonight.

MOTHER: No, you didn't.

ALBERT *exclaims and knots the tie.*

I thought you were joking.

ALBERT: I'm not going . . . I'm just going to Mr. King's. I've told you. You don't believe me.

MOTHER: You're going to Mr. King's?

ALBERT: Mr. Ryan's leaving. You know Ryan. He's leaving the firm. He's been there years. So Mr. King's giving a sort of party for him at his house . . . well, not exactly a party, not a party, just a few . . . you know . . . anyway, we're all invited. I've got to go. Everyone else is going. I've got to go. I don't want to go, but I've got to.

MOTHER [*bewildered, sitting*]: Well, I don't know . . .

ALBERT [*with his arm round her*]: I won't be late. I don't want to go. I'd much rather stay with you.

MOTHER: Would you?

ALBERT: You know I would. Who wants to go to Mr. King's party?

MOTHER: We were going to have our game of cards.

ALBERT: Well, we can't have our game of cards.

[*Pause.*]

MOTHER: Put the bulb in Grandma's room, Albert.

ALBERT: I've told you I'm not going down to the cellar in my white shirt. There's no light in the cellar either. I'll be pitch black in five minutes, looking for those bulbs.

MOTHER: I told you to put a light in the cellar. I told you yesterday.

ALBERT: Well, I can't do it now.

MOTHER: If we had a light in the cellar you'd be able to see where those bulbs were. You don't expect me to go down to the cellar?

ALBERT: I don't know why we keep bulbs in the cellar!

[*Pause.*]

MOTHER: Your father would turn in his grave if he heard you raise your voice to me. You're all I've got, Albert. I want you to remember that. I haven't got anyone else. I want you . . . I want you to bear that in mind.

ALBERT: I'm sorry . . . I raised my voice.

He goes to the door.

[*Mumbling.*] I've got to go.

MOTHER [*following*]: Albert!

ALBERT: What?

MOTHER: I want to ask you a question.

ALBERT: What?

MOTHER: Are you leading a clean life?

ALBERT: A clean life?

MOTHER: You're not leading an unclean life, are you?

ALBERT: What are you talking about?

MOTHER: You're not messing about with girls, are you? You're not going to go messing about with girls tonight?

ALBERT: Don't be so ridiculous.

MOTHER: Answer me, Albert. I'm your mother.

ALBERT: I don't know any girls.

MOTHER: If you're going to the firm's party, there'll be girls there, won't there? Girls from the office?

ALBERT: I don't like them, any of them.

MOTHER: You promise?

ALBERT: Promise what?

MOTHER: That . . . that you won't upset your father.

ALBERT: My father? How can I upset my father? You're always talking about upsetting people who are dead!

MOTHER: Oh, Albert, you don't know how you hurt me, you don't know the hurtful way you've got, speaking of your poor father like that.

ALBERT: But he is dead.

MOTHER: He's not! He's living! [*Touching her breast.*] In here! And this is his house!

[*Pause.*]

ALBERT: Look, Mum, I won't be late . . . and I won't . . .

MOTHER: But what about your dinner? It's nearly ready.

ALBERT: Seeley and Kedge are waiting for me. I told you not to cook dinner this morning. [*He goes to the stairs.*] Just because you never listen . . .

He runs up the stairs and disappears. She calls after him from the hall.

MOTHER: Well, what am I going to do while you're out? I can't go into Grandma's room because there's no light. I can't go down to the cellar in the dark, we were going to have a game of cards, it's Friday night, what about our game of rummy?

SCENE TWO

A coffee stall by a railway arch. A wooden bench is situated a short distance from it.

SEELEY *and* KEDGE, *both about* ALBERT'S *age, are at the counter, talking to the barman. An old man leans at the corner of the counter.*

SEELEY: Give us a cheese roll as well, will you?

KEDGE: Make it two.

SEELEY: Make it two.

BARMAN: Two cheese rolls.

SEELEY: What are these, sausages?

BARMAN: Best pork sausages.

SEELEY [*to* KEDGE]: You want a sausage?

KEDGE [*shuddering*]: No, thanks.

SEELEY: Yes, you're right.

BARMAN: Two cheese rolls. What about these sausages, you want them or don't you?

SEELEY: Just the rolls, mate.

BARMAN: Two tea, two rolls, makes one and eightpence.

SEELEY *gives him half a crown.*

KEDGE: There'll be plenty to eat at the party.

SEELEY: I'll bet.

OLD MAN: Eh! [*They turn to him.*] Your mate was by here not long ago.

SEELEY: Which mate?

OLD MAN: He had a cup of tea, didn't he, Fred? Sitting over there he was, on the bench. He said he was going home to change but to tell you he'd be back.

KEDGE: Uh-uh.

OLD MAN: Not gone more than above forty-five minutes.

BARMAN: One and eight from half a dollar leaves you ten pennies.

OLD MAN: Anyway, he told me to tell you when I see you he was coming back.

KEDGE: Thanks very much.

SEELEY: Well, I hope he won't be long. I don't want to miss the booze.

KEDGE: You think there'll be much there, do you?

OLD MAN: Yes, he was sitting over there.

KEDGE: Who was?

OLD MAN: Your mate.

SEELEY: Oh yes.

OLD MAN: Yes, sitting over there he was. Took his cup of tea and went and sat down, didn't he, Fred? He sat there looking very compressed with himself.

KEDGE: Very what?

OLD MAN: Compressed. I thought he was looking compressed, didn't you, Fred?

BARMAN: Depressed. He means depressed.

SEELEY: No wonder. What about that game on Saturday, eh?

KEDGE: You were going to tell me. You haven't told me yet.

BARMAN: What game? Fulham?

SEELEY: No, the firm. Firm's got a team, see? Play on Saturdays.

BARMAN: Who'd you play?

SEELEY: Other firms.

BARMAN: You boys in the team, are you?

KEDGE: Yes. I've been off sick though. I didn't play last week.

BARMAN: Sick, eh? You want to try one of my sausages, don't he, Henry?

OLD MAN: Oh, ay, yes.

KEDGE: What happened with the game, then?

They move to the bench.

SEELEY: Well, when you couldn't play, Gidney moved Albert to left back.

KEDGE: He's a left half.

SEELEY: I know he's a left half. I said to Gidney myself, I said to him, look, why don't you go left back, Gidney? He said, no, I'm too valuable at centre half.

KEDGE: He didn't, did he?

SEELEY: Yes. Well, you know who was on the right wing, don't you? Connor.

KEDGE: Who? Tony Connor?

SEELEY: No. You know Connor. What's the matter with you? You've played against Connor yourself.

KEDGE: Oh—whatsisname—Micky Connor.

SEELEY: Yes.

KEDGE: I thought he'd given up the game.

SEELEY: No, what are you talking about? He plays for the printing works, plays outside right for the printing works.

KEDGE: He's a good ballplayer, that Connor, isn't he?

SEELEY: Look. I said to Albert before the kick off, Connor's on the right wing, I said, play your normal game. I told him six times before the kick off.

KEDGE: What's the good of him playing his normal game? He's a left half, he's not a left back.

SEELEY: Yes, but he's a defensive left half, isn't he? That's why I told him to play his normal game. You don't want to worry about Connor, I said, he's a good ballplayer but he's not all that good.

KEDGE: Oh, he's good, though.

SEELEY: No one's denying he's good. But he's not all that good. I mean, he's not tip-top. You know what I mean?

KEDGE: He's fast.

SEELEY: He's fast, but he's not all that fast, is he?

KEDGE [*doubtfully*]: Well, not all that fast . . .

SEELEY: What about Levy? Was Levy fast?

KEDGE: Well, Levy was a sprinter.

SEELEY: He was a dasher, Levy. All he knew was run.

KEDGE: He could move.

SEELEY: Yes, but look how Albert played him! He cut him off, he played him out the game. And Levy's faster than Connor.

KEDGE: Yes, but he wasn't so clever, though.

SEELEY: Well, what about Foxall?

KEDGE: Who? Lou Foxall?

SEELEY: No, you're talking about Lou Fox, I'm talking about Sandy Foxall.

KEDGE: Oh, the winger.

SEELEY: Sure. He was a very smart ballplayer, Foxall. But what did Albert do? He played his normal game. He let him come. He waited for him. And Connor's not as clever as Foxall.

KEDGE: He's clever though.

SEELEY: Gawd blimey, I know he's clever, but he's not as clever as Foxall, is he?

KEDGE: The trouble is, with Connor, he's fast too, isn't he?

SEELEY: But if Albert would have played his normal game! He played a game foreign to him.

KEDGE: How many'd Connor get?

SEELEY: He made three and scored two.

Pause. They eat.

KEDGE: No wonder he's depressed, old Albert.

SEELEY: Oh, he was very depressed after the game, I can tell you. And of course Gidney was after him, of course. You know Gidney.

KEDGE: That birk.

[*Pause.*]

OLD MAN: Yes, he was sitting over where you are now, wasn't he, Fred? Looking very compressed with himself. Light-haired bloke, ain't he?

SEELEY: Yes, light-haired.

SCENE THREE

The house.

ALBERT *is coming down the stairs. He is wearing his jacket. He goes towards the door. His mother calls from the kitchen and goes into the hall.*

MOTHER: Albert! Where are you going?

ALBERT: Out.

MOTHER: Your dinner's ready.

ALBERT: I'm sorry. I haven't got time to have it.

MOTHER: Look at your suit. You're not going out with your suit in that state, are you?

ALBERT: What's the matter with it?

MOTHER: It needs a good brush, that's what's the matter with it. You can't go out like that. Come on, come in here and I'll give it a brush.

ALBERT: It's all right . . .

MOTHER: Come on.

They go into the kitchen. She gets the brush.

Turn round. No, stand still. You can't go out and disgrace me, Albert. If you've got to go out you've got to look nice. There, that's better.

She dusts his jacket with her hands and straightens his tie.

I didn't tell you what I made for you, did I? I made it specially. I made Shepherd's Pie tonight.

ALBERT [*taking her hand from his tie*]: The tie's all right.

He goes to the door.

Well, ta-ta.

MOTHER: Albert! Wait a minute. Where's your handkerchief?

ALBERT: What handkerchief?

MOTHER: You haven't got a handkerchief in your breast pocket.

ALBERT: That doesn't matter, does it?

MOTHER: Doesn't matter? I should say it does matter. Just a minute. [*She takes a handkerchief from a drawer.*] Here you are. A nice clean one. [*She arranges it in his pocket.*] You mustn't let me down, you know. You've got to be properly dressed. Your father was always properly dressed. You'd never see him out without a handkerchief in his breast pocket. He always looked like a gentleman.

SCENE FOUR

The coffee stall.
KEDGE *is returning from the counter with two teas.*

KEDGE: Time we were there.

SEELEY: We'll give him five minutes.

KEDGE: I bet his Mum's combing his hair for him, eh?

He chuckles and sits.

You ever met her, Seeley?

SEELEY: Who?

KEDGE: His . . . mother.

SEELEY: Yes.

KEDGE: What's she like?

SEELEY [*shortly*]: She's all right.

KEDGE: All right, is she?

SEELEY: I told you. I just said she was all right.

[*Pause.*]

KEDGE: No, what I mean is, he always gets a bit niggly when she's mentioned, doesn't he? A bit touchy. You noticed that?

SEELEY [*unwillingly*]: Yes.

KEDGE: Why's that, then?

SEELEY: I don't know. What're you asking me for?

KEDGE: I don't know. I just thought you might . . . sort of . . . well, I mean, you know him better than I do, don't you? [*Pause.*]

Of course, he don't let much slip, does he, old Albert?

SEELEY: No, not much.

KEDGE: He's a bit deep really, isn't he?

SEELEY: Yes, he's a bit deep.

[*Pause.*]

KEDGE: Secretive.

SEELEY [*irritably*]: What do you mean, secretive? What are you talking about?

KEDGE: I was just saying he was secretive.

SEELEY: What are you talking about? What do you mean, he's secretive?

KEDGE: You said yourself he was deep.

SEELEY: I said he was deep. I didn't say he was secretive!

ALBERT *walks through the railway arch across to the bench.*

KEDGE: Hullo, Albert.

ALBERT: Hullo.

KEDGE: That's a nice bit of clobber you've got on there.

SEELEY: Very fair, very fair.

KEDGE: Yes, fits you like a glove.

SEELEY: Well, come on, catch a thirty-six round the corner.

ALBERT: Wait a minute, I . . . I don't think I feel like going, actually.

KEDGE: What are you talking about?

ALBERT: I don't feel like it, that's all.

SEELEY: What, with all that drink laid on?

ALBERT: No, I've just got a bit of a headache.

OLD MAN: That's the bloke! That's the bloke was here before, isn't it, Fred? I gave them your message, son.

ALBERT: Oh . . . thanks.

OLD MAN: Didn't I?

KEDGE: You did, you did, mate.

SEELEY: Well, what's going on, you coming or what?

ALBERT [touching his forehead]: No, I feel a bit . . . you know . . .

KEDGE: Don't you know who'll be there tonight, Albert?

ALBERT: Who?

KEDGE: Joyce.

ALBERT: Joyce? Well, what about it?

KEDGE: And Eileen.

ALBERT: Well, so what?

KEDGE: And Betty. Betty'll be there. They'll all be there.

SEELEY: Betty? Who's Betty?

KEDGE: Betty? What do you mean? You don't know Betty?

SEELEY: There's no girl in the office called Betty.

KEDGE: Betty! The dark bit! The new one. The one that came in last week. The little one, in the corner!

SEELEY: Oh, her. Is her name Betty? I thought it was—

KEDGE: Betty. Her name's Betty.

SEELEY: I've been calling her Hetty.

[Pause.]

KEDGE: Anywhat, she'll be there. She's raring to go, that one.

ALBERT: Well, you go then, I'll . . .

KEDGE: Albert, what's the matter with you, mate? It's wine, women and song tonight.

ALBERT: I see them every day, don't I? What's new in that?

KEDGE: You frightened Gidney'll be after you, then, because of the game?

ALBERT: What do you mean?

KEDGE: Go on, everyone has a bad game, Albert.

ALBERT: Yes, they do, don't they?

KEDGE: I played against Connor myself once. He's tricky. He's a very tricky ballplayer.

ALBERT: Yes.

SEELEY: Clever player, Connor.

ALBERT: What's Gidney got to do with it, Kedge?

KEDGE: Well, you know what he is.

ALBERT: What?

KEDGE: Well, he's captain of the team, isn't he, for a bang-off?

ALBERT: You think—?

SEELEY: Oh, scrub round it, will you? It's late—

ALBERT: You think I'm frightened of Gidney?

KEDGE: I didn't say you were—

SEELEY: Gidney's all right. What's the matter with Gidney?

ALBERT: Yes. What's wrong with him?

KEDGE: Nothing. There's nothing wrong with him. He's a nice bloke. He's a charmer, isn't he?

SEELEY: The cream of the cream. Well, come on, you coming or what?

ALBERT: Yes, all right. I'll come.

SEELEY: Just a minute. I'll get some fags.

He goes to the counter. ALBERT *and* KEDGE *are left standing.*

[*To the* BARMAN.] Twenty 'Weights', mate.

KEDGE *regards* ALBERT.

KEDGE: How's your Mum, Albert?

ALBERT: All right.

KEDGE: That's the idea.

BARMAN: Only got 'Woods'.

SEELEY: They'll do.

ALBERT [*quietly*]: What do you mean, how's my Mum?

KEDGE: I just asked how she was, that's all.

ALBERT: Why shouldn't she be all right?

KEDGE: I didn't say she wasn't.

ALBERT: Well, she is.

KEDGE: Well, that's all right then, isn't it?

ALBERT: What are you getting at?

KEDGE: I don't know what's the matter with you tonight, Albert.

SEELEY [*returning*]: What's up now?

ALBERT: Kedge here, suddenly asks how my mother is.

KEDGE: Just a friendly question, that's all. Gaw! You can't even ask a bloke how his mother is now without him getting niggly!

ALBERT: Well, why's he suddenly ask—?

SEELEY: He was just asking a friendly question, mate. What's the matter with you?

[*Pause*]

ALBERT: Oh.

SEELEY: Well, how is she, then?

ALBERT: She's fine. What about yours?

SEELEY: Fine. Fine.

[*Pause.*]

KEDGE: Mine's fine too, you know. Great. Absolutely great. A marvel for her age, my mother is. Of course, she had me very late.

[*Pause.*]

SEELEY: Well? Are you coming or not? Or what?

KEDGE: I'm coming.

ALBERT [*following*]: I'm coming.

SCENE FIVE

The kitchen. The MOTHER *is putting* ALBERT'S *dinner into the oven. She takes the alarm clock from the mantelpiece and puts it on the table. She takes out a pack of cards, sits at the table and begins to lay out a game of patience. Close up of her, broodingly setting out the cards. Close up of the clock. It is seven forty-five.*

Act Two

SCENE ONE

The lounge of MR. KING'S *house. The party is in progress.*
KEDGE *and* BETTY *are dancing. Music comes from a radio-gram.* MR. KING, *an urbane man in his fifties,* GIDNEY, *the chief accountant, in his late twenties,* SEELEY *and* ALBERT, *are standing in a group.* JOYCE *and* EILEEN *are at the table which serves as a bar. Two men and a woman of indeterminate age sit holding drinks.* HORNE *and* BARROW, *two young clerks, stand by the door.* MR. RYAN, *the old man, sits in the centre of the room, smiling.*

JOYCE: You enjoying the party, Mr. Ryan?

RYAN *nods and smiles.*

EILEEN [*pleasantly*]: Enjoying the party, are you?

He nods, winks and smiles.

KING: I recommend a bicycle, honestly. It really keeps you up to the mark. Out in the morning, on the bike, through the town . . . the air in your lungs, muscles working . . . you arrive at work . . . you arrive at work fresh . . . you know what I mean? Uplifted.

GIDNEY: Not so good in the rain.

KING: Refreshes you! Clears the cobwebs. [*He laughs.*]

SEELEY: You don't walk to work, do you, Gidney?

GIDNEY: Me? I've got the car.

KING: I drive too, of course, but I often think seriously of taking up cycling again. I often think very seriously about it, you know.

JOYCE [*to* RYAN]: Nice party, isn't it, Mr. Ryan?

RYAN *nods and inclines his head, smiling*.

KEDGE [*dancing*]: You dance like a dream, Betty, you know that?

BETTY [*shyly*]: I don't.

KEDGE: You do. Honest. Like a dream. Like a dream come true.

BETTY: You're just saying that.

KING: Well, Kedge looks all right again, doesn't he? What was the matter with him? I've forgotten.

SEELEY: Stomach trouble.

KING: Not enough exercise. [*To* KEDGE.] You'll have to see you get more exercise, Kedge!

KEDGE [*passing*]: You never said a truer word, Mr. King.

SEELEY: Well, he don't look in bad trim to me, Mr. King.

They laugh.

KING: I must admit it.

GIDNEY: He'll never get to the last lap with that one, I can tell you.

KING [*smiling*]: Now, now, you young men, that's quite enough of that. No more of that.

GIDNEY [*pleasantly*]: What are you laughing at, Stokes?

ALBERT: What?

GIDNEY: Sorry. I thought you were laughing.

ALBERT: I was laughing. You made a joke.

GIDNEY: Oh yes, of course. Sorry.

[*Pause.*]

Well, we've got Kedge back at left back next Saturday.

KING: Yes. Excuse me.

SEELEY: That's a lovely pair of shoes you're wearing, Gidney.

GIDNEY: Do you think so?

SEELEY: Oh, they're the best, the very best, aren't they, Albert? Gidney always wears a nice pair of shoes, doesn't he, you noticed that? That's one thing I'll say about you, Gidney—you carry your feet well.

EILEEN: A mambo! Who's going to dance?

SEELEY: I'll give it a trot.

SEELEY *and* EILEEN *dance.*

GIDNEY: Don't you dance, Stokes?

ALBERT: Yes, sometimes.

GIDNEY: Do you? You will excuse me, won't you?

ALBERT: Yes.

ALBERT *is left standing.*

KING: Well, Ryan, enjoying the party?

RYAN *nods, smiles.*

Nice to see a lot of young people enjoying themselves, eh?

RYAN *nods, smiles.*

Of course, it's all in your honour, old man. Let's fill you up. I'll be the oldest man in the office after you've gone.

GIDNEY *and* JOYCE, *whispering.*

JOYCE: No. Why should I?

GIDNEY: Go on. Just for a lark.

JOYCE: What for?

GIDNEY: For a lark. Just for a lark.

JOYCE: You've got an evil mind, you have.

GIDNEY: No, it'll amuse me, that's all. I feel like being amused.

JOYCE: Well, I'm not going to.

GIDNEY: Gah, you wouldn't know how to, anyway.

JOYCE: Oh, wouldn't I?

GIDNEY [*taking her arm*]: Get hold of Eileen, don't tell her I
  told you though, and go over and lead him a dance, just
  lead him a dance, that's all, see what he does. I want to
  see his reaction, that's all, I just want to see how he
  takes it.

JOYCE: What, in front of everyone else, in front of—?

GIDNEY: Just talk to him, talk to him. I don't mean anything
  else, do I?

JOYCE: What do I get if I do?

GIDNEY: A toffee apple.

JOYCE: Oh, really? Thank you.

GIDNEY: I'll take you for a ride in the car. Honest.

SEELEY [*dancing*]: Hullo, Mr. Ryan. Enjoying the party?

EILEEN: You dance well, don't you?

SEELEY: I was going in for ballet once.

EILEEN: Go on!

SEELEY: Yes, true. They offered me the leading part in
  Rigoletto. When I was a boy soprano.

EILEEN: You're making it up.

GIDNEY [*to* JOYCE]: No, he just irritates me, that bloke. I
  . . . I haven't got any time for a bloke like that.

JOYCE: He's just quiet, that's all.

GIDNEY: Well, see if you can wake him up.

KING [*to* BETTY]: Well, Miss Todd, it hasn't taken you long
  to get to know everyone, has it?

BETTY: Oh no, Mr. King.

KEDGE: I've taken her under my wing, Mr. King.

KING: So I noticed.

KEDGE: Yes, I've been teaching her all about mortality tables.
  I told her in case of fire or burglary commission and
  damages come to her.

KING: I would hardly take Kedge's word as gospel, Miss
  Todd.

KEDGE: You know I've got the best interests of the firm at
  heart, Mr. King.

GIDNEY [*drinking, with* JOYCE]: Anyway, I'm thinking of moving on. You stay too long in a place you go daft. After all, with my qualifications I could go anywhere.

He sees ALBERT *at the bar.*

Couldn't I, Stokes?

ALBERT: What?

GIDNEY: I was saying, with my qualifications I could go anywhere. I could go anywhere and be anything.

ALBERT: So could I.

GIDNEY: Could you? What qualifications have you got?

ALBERT: Well, I've got a few, you know.

GIDNEY: Listen! Do you know that Chelsea wanted to sign me up a few years ago? They had a scout down to one of our games. They wanted to sign me up. And I'll tell you another thing as well. I could turn professional cricketer any day I wanted to, if I wanted to.

ALBERT: Then why don't you?

GIDNEY: I don't want to.

JOYCE: You'd look lovely in white.

GIDNEY: These people who talk about qualifications. Just makes me laugh, that's all.

KEDGE [*in the corner of the room, in an armchair with* BETTY]: Oh, you're lovely. You're the loveliest thing on four wheels.

KING [*to* HORNE *and* BARROW, *by the door*]: Well, I hope you'll both be in the team soon yourselves. I think it's a very good thing we've . . . that the firm's got a football team. And a cricket team, of course. It shows we look on the lighter side of things too. Don't you agree?

HORNE: Oh yes, Mr. King.

BARROW: Yes, Mr. King.

KING: Also gives a sense of belonging. Work together and play together. Office work can become so impersonal. We like to foster . . . to foster something . . . very different. You know what I mean?

HORNE: Oh yes, Mr. King.

BARROW: Yes, Mr. King.

KING: You interested in sailing, by any chance? You're quite welcome to come down to my boat at Poole any weekend—do a bit of sailing along the coast.

HORNE: Oh, thank you, Mr. King.

BARROW: Thank you, Mr. King.

JOYCE *and* EILEEN, *whispering.*

JOYCE [*slyly*]: Eh, what about going over and cheering up old Albert?

EILEEN: What for?

JOYCE: Well, he looks a bit gloomy, don't he?

EILEEN: I don't want to go over. You go over.

JOYCE: No, come on. You come over.

EILEEN: What for?

JOYCE: Cheer him up. For a bit of fun.

EILEEN: Oh, you're awful.

JOYCE: Come on. Come over.

KING [*to* RYAN]: Can I fill your glass, Ryan?

[RYAN *nods, and smiles.*]

Can't leave you without a drink, can we? The guest of honour.

JOYCE *and* EILEEN *sit either side of* ALBERT *on a divan.*

JOYCE: Mind if we join you?

ALBERT: Oh, hullo.

EILEEN: Enjoying the party?

JOYCE: What are you sitting all gloomy about?

ALBERT: I'm not gloomy, I'm just sitting, drinking. Feel a bit tired, actually.

JOYCE: Why, what have you been doing?

ALBERT: Nothing.

JOYCE: You just said you were tired. Eh, move up, I'm on the edge.

ALBERT: Sorry.

EILEEN: Eh, mind out, you're squashing me.

ALBERT: Oh . . .

JOYCE: You squash her, she won't mind.

EILEEN [*laughing*]: Oh, Joyce!

GIDNEY, *with a smile, watching.*

JOYCE: Come on, tell us, what are you tired about?

ALBERT: Oh, just work, I suppose.

JOYCE: I've been working too. I'm not tired. I love work. Don't you, Eileen? [*She leans across him to speak.*]

EILEEN: Oh yes, I love work.

ALBERT: No, I'm not tired, really. I'm all right.

EILEEN: He looks tired.

JOYCE: You've been living it up. Women.

EILEEN: I'll bet.

JOYCE: Females.

The girls giggle.

ALBERT [*with an uncertain smile*]: No, I wouldn't . . .

EILEEN: Eh, mind your drink. My best taffeta.

JOYCE: He's not bad looking when you get close.

EILEEN: Quite nice when you get close.

ALBERT: Thanks for the compliment.

EILEEN: You got a flat of your own?

ALBERT: No. Have you?

EILEEN [*forlornly*]: No.

JOYCE: You live with your mother, don't you?

ALBERT: Yes.

JOYCE: Does she look after you all right, then?

ALBERT: Yes, she . . . [*He stands.*] I'm just going to the bar.

JOYCE: So are we.

EILEEN: Me too.

They follow.

KING: Well, now everyone . . .

JOYCE: I'm having gin.

ALBERT: Gin? Wait a minute . . .

KING: Just a minute, everyone, can I have your attention?

GIDNEY [to JOYCE]: Didn't make much impression, did you?

JOYCE: Didn't I?

KING: Just for a moment, please . . .

GIDNEY: Eh, Stokes, pay attention, will you?

ALBERT: What?

GIDNEY: Mr. King wants your attention.

KING: I'd just like to propose a toast to our guest of honour, Mr. Ryan. Gidney!

GIDNEY: Yes?

ALBERT: Here's your gin, then.

JOYCE: Thanks.

KING [to GIDNEY]: Go and get Kedge out of that corner, will you? Now, as you know, we're all gathered here tonight to pay our respects to our old friend and colleague, Mr. Ryan . . .

KEDGE and BETTY are locked together in the armchair. GIDNEY taps KEDGE on the shoulder.

GIDNEY: Mr. King wants to know if you'll honour the party with your presence.

KEDGE [jumping up]: Oh, sorry. [BETTY, thrown off, falls. He picks her up.] Sorry.

KING: We've all known Mr. Ryan for a very long time. Of course, I've known him myself much longer than anyone here—

KEDGE: For he's a jolly good fellow—

KING: Wait! Very glad for your enthusiasm, Mr. Kedge. Your heart, I am quite sure, is in the right place.

General laughter.

ALBERT, EILEEN, JOYCE, SEELEY and GIDNEY stand in a group around MR. RYAN'S chair.

But please allow me to toast Mr. Ryan first and then the floor is yours. Well, as I was saying, the whole department is here tonight to pay tribute to a man who from time immemorial has become, how shall I put it, the very core of our little community. I remember Mr. Ryan sitting at his very own desk the first time my father brought me into the office—

A sharp scream and stiffening from EILEEN. *All turn to her.*

Good heavens!

GIDNEY: What is it?

AD LIB: What's happened? Eileen, what's the matter?

EILEEN: Someone touched me!

JOYCE: Touched you?

EILEEN: Someone touched me! Someone—!

BETTY: What did he do?

KEDGE: Touched you? What did he do?

JOYCE: What did he do, Eileen?

EILEEN: He . . . he . . . he took a liberty!

KEDGE: Go on! Who did?

EILEEN *turns and stares at* ALBERT. *Silence. All stare at* ALBERT.

ALBERT: What are you looking at me for?

GIDNEY [*muttering*]: Good God . . .

Tense, embarrassed pause.

HORNE [*at the door, whispering*]: What did he do, touch her?

BARROW [*open-mouthed*]: Yes.

HORNE [*wide-eyed*]: Where?

They look at each other, open-mouthed and wide-eyed.

ALBERT: What are you looking at me for?

KING: Please, now . . . can we possibly . . . I mean . . .

EILEEN [*in a voice of reproach, indignation and horror*]: Albert!

ALBERT: What do you mean?

SEELEY: How does she know it was Albert?

KEDGE: Wonder what he did. Made her jump didn't he?

ALBERT: Now look, wait a minute, this is absolutely ridiculous—

GIDNEY: Ridiculous, eh? I'll say it is. What do you think you're up to?

EILEEN: Yes, I was just standing there, suddenly this hand . . .

JOYCE: I could tell he was that sort.

The camera closes on MR. RYAN'S *hand, resting comfortably on his knee, and then to his face which, smiling vaguely, is inclined to the ceiling. It must be quite clear from the expression that it was his hand which strayed.*

GIDNEY: Come out here, Albert.

ALBERT: Don't pull me. What are you doing?

SEELEY: How do you know it was him?

ALBERT [*throwing off* GIDNEY'S *hand*]: Let go of me!

SEELEY: What are you pulling him for?

GIDNEY: You keep out of this.

KING [*nervously*]: Now please let me continue my toast, ladies and gentlemen. Really, you must settle this elsewhere.

SEELEY: We don't even know what he's supposed to have done.

ALBERT: I didn't do anything.

GIDNEY: We can guess what he did.

KING [*at speed*]: We are all collected here tonight in honour of Mr. Ryan and to present him with a token of our affection—

JOYCE [*to* ALBERT]: You snake!

SEELEY: Well, what did he do? What's he supposed to have done?

ALBERT: She doesn't know what she's talking about.

SEELEY: Come on, what's he supposed to have done, Eileen, anyway?

EILEEN: Mind you own business.

JOYCE: You don't think she's going to tell you, do you?

GIDNEY: Look, Seeley, why don't you shut up?

SEELEY: Now don't talk to me like that, Gidney.

ALBERT: Don't worry about him, Seeley.

KING: As I have been trying to say—

JOYCE: You come over here, Eileen, sit down. She's upset, aren't you?

EILEEN [to SEELEY]: So would you be!

KING: Miss Phipps, would you mind composing yourself?

EILEEN: Composing myself!

GIDNEY: Come outside a minute, Albert.

KING: As I have been trying to say—

KEDGE [brightly]: I'm listening, Mr. King!

KING: What?

KEDGE: I'm listening. I'm with you.

KING: Oh, thank you. Thank you, my boy.

ALBERT: I'm going, anyway.

ALBERT *goes into the hall, followed by* GIDNEY *and* SEELEY. *The door shuts behind them.*

GIDNEY: Wait a minute, Stokes.

ALBERT: What do you want?

GIDNEY: I haven't been satisfied with your . . . sort of . . . behaviour for some time, you know that, don't you?

ALBERT: You haven't . . . you haven't what?

GIDNEY: For instance, there was that bloody awful game of football you played when you threw the game away last Saturday that I've got on my mind, besides one or two other things!

SEELEY: Eh look, Gidney, you're talking like a prize—

GIDNEY [viciously]: I've told you to keep out of this.

ALBERT [tensely]: I'm going, anyway.

GIDNEY: Wait a minute, let's have it out. What do you think you're up to?

ALBERT: Look, I've told you—

GIDNEY: What did you think you were doing with that girl?

ALBERT: I didn't touch her.

GIDNEY: I'm responsible for that girl. She's a good friend of mine. I know her uncle.

ALBERT: Do you?

SEELEY: You know, you're being so stupid, Gidney—

GIDNEY: Seeley, I can take you any day, you know that, don't you?

SEELEY: Go on!

GIDNEY: Any day.

SEELEY: You can take me any day?

GIDNEY: Any day.

SEELEY: Well, go on, then. Go on . . . if you can take me . . .

ALBERT: Seeley—

SEELEY: No, if he says he can take me, if he can take me any day . . .

The door opens slightly. HORNE *and* BARROW *peer out.*

ALBERT: Gidney, why don't you . . . why don't you get back to the party?

GIDNEY: I was telling you, Albert—

ALBERT: Stokes.

GIDNEY: I was telling you, Albert, that if you're going to behave like a boy of ten in mixed company—

ALBERT: I told you my name's Stokes!

GIDNEY: Don't be childish, Albert.

A sudden silence. MR. KING'S *voice from the room.*

KING: . . . and for his unfailing good humour and cheeriness, Mr. Ryan will always be remembered at Hislop, King and Martindale!

Scattered applause. HORNE, *caught by their stares, shuts the door hastily.*

ALBERT [*going to the door*.]: Goodnight.

GIDNEY [*obstructing him*]: Go back and apologize.

ALBERT: What for?

GIDNEY: For insulting a lady. Mate. A lady. Something to do with breeding. But I suppose you're too bloody backward to know anything about that.

ALBERT: You're talking right out of your hat.

SEELEY: Right out of the bowler.

GIDNEY [*to* SEELEY]: No one invited you out here, did they?

SEELEY: Who invited you?

GIDNEY: I'm talking to this man on behalf of the firm! Unless I get a satisfactory explanation I shall think seriously about recommending his dismissal.

ALBERT: Get out of my way, will you?

GIDNEY: Acting like an animal all over the place—

ALBERT: Move out of it!

GIDNEY [*breathlessly*]: I know your trouble.

ALBERT: Oh, yes?

GIDNEY: Yes, sticks out a mile.

ALBERT: Does it?

GIDNEY: Yes.

ALBERT: What's my trouble then?

GIDNEY [*very deliberately*]: You're a mother's boy. That's what you are. That's your trouble. You're a mother's boy.

ALBERT *hits him. There is a scuffle.* SEELEY *tries to part them. The three rock back and forth in the hall: confused blows, words and grunts.*

The door of the room opens. Faces. MR. KING *comes out.*

KING: What in heaven's name is going on here!

The scuffle stops. A short silence. ALBERT *opens the front door, goes out and slams it behind him. He stands on the doorstep, breathing heavily, his face set.*

SCENE TWO

The kitchen.

MRS. STOKES *is asleep, her head resting on the table, the cards
disordered. The clock ticks. It is twelve o'clock. The front
door opens slowly.* ALBERT *comes in, closes the door softly,
stops, looks across to the open kitchen door, sees his mother,
and begins to creep up the stairs with great stealth. The camera
follows him. Her voice stops him.*

MOTHER: Albert!

He stops.

Albert! Is that you?

She goes to the kitchen door.

What are you creeping up the stairs for? Might have been
a burglar. What would I have done then?

He descends slowly.

Creeping up the stairs like that. Give anyone a fright.
Creeping up the stairs like that. You leave me in the house
all alone . . . [*She stops and regards him.*] Look at you!
Look at your suit. What's the matter with your tie, it's all
crumpled, I pressed it for you this morning. Well, I won't
even ask any questions. That's all. You look a disgrace.

*He walks past her into the kitchen, goes to the sink and
pours himself a glass of water. She follows him.*

What have you been doing, mucking about with girls?

She begins to pile the cards.

Mucking about with girls, I suppose. Do you know what
the time is? I fell asleep, right here at this table, waiting

for you. I don't know what your father would say. Coming in this time of night. It's after twelve o'clock. In a state like that. Drunk, I suppose. I suppose your dinner's ruined. Well, if you want to make a convenience out of your own home, that's your business. I'm only your mother, I don't suppose that counts for much these days. I'm not saying any more. If you want to go mucking about with girls, that's your business.

She takes his dinner out of the oven.

Well, anyway, you'll have your dinner. You haven't eaten a single thing all night.

She places a plate on the table and gets knife and fork. He stands by the sink, sipping water.

I wouldn't mind if you found a really nice girl and brought her home and introduced her to your mother, brought her home for dinner, I'd know you were sincere, if she was a really nice girl, she'd be like a daughter to me. But you've never brought a girl home here in your life. I suppose you're ashamed of your mother.
[*Pause.*]
Come on, it's all dried up. I kept it on a low light. I couldn't even go up to Grandma's room and have a look round because there wasn't any bulb, you might as well eat it.

He stands.

What's the matter, are you drunk? Where did you go, to one of those pubs in the West End? You'll get into serious trouble, my boy, if you frequent those places, I'm warning you. Don't you read the papers?
[*Pause.*]
I hope you're satisfied, anyway. The house in darkness, I wasn't going to break my neck going down to that cellar

to look for a bulb, you come home looking like I don't
know what, anyone would think you gave me a fortune out
of your wages. Yes. I don't say anything, do I? I keep
quiet about what you expect me to manage on. I never
grumble. I keep a lovely home, I bet there's none of the
boys in your firm better fed than you are. I'm not asking for
gratitude. But one things hurts me, Albert, and I'll tell
you what it is. Not for years, not for years, have you come
up to me and said, Mum, I love you, like you did when you
were a little boy. You've never said it without me having to
ask you. Not since before your father died. And he was a
good man. He had high hopes of you. I've never told you,
Albert, about the high hopes he had of you. I don't know
what you do with all your money. But don't forget what it
cost us to rear you, my boy, I've never told you about the
sacrifices we made, you wouldn't care, anyway. Telling me
lies about going to the firm's party. They've got a bit of
respect at that firm, that's why we sent you there, to start
off your career, they wouldn't let you carry on like that at
one of their functions. Mr. King would have his eye on you.
I don't know where you've been. Well, if you don't want
to lead a clean life it's your lookout, if you want to go
mucking about with all sorts of bits of girls, if you're content to leave your own mother sitting here till midnight,
and I wasn't feeling well, anyway, I didn't tell you because
I didn't want to upset you, I keep things from you, you're
the only one I've got, but what do you care, you don't care,
you don't care, the least you can do is sit down and eat the
dinner I cooked for you, specially for you, it's Shepherd's
Pie—

ALBERT *lunges to the table, picks up the clock and violently
raises it above his head. A stifled scream from the* MOTHER.

Act Three

SCENE ONE

The coffee stall, shuttered.

ALBERT *is leaning against it. He is sweating. He is holding the butt of a cigarette. There is a sound of a foot on gravel. He starts, the butt burns his hand, he drops it and turns. A* GIRL *is looking at him. She smiles.*

GIRL: Good evening.
   [*Pause.*]
   What are you doing?
   [*Pause.*]
   What are you doing out at this time of night?

   She moves closer to him.

   I live just round the corner.

   He stares at her.

   Like to? Chilly out here, isn't it? Come on.
   [*Pause.*]
   Come on.

   He goes with her.

SCENE TWO

The GIRL'S *room. The door opens. She comes in. Her manner has changed from the seductive. She is brisk and nervous.*

GIRL: Come in. Don't slam the door. Shut it gently. I'll light the fire. Chilly out, don't you find? Have you got a match?

He walks across the room.

GIRL: Please don't walk so heavily. Please. There's no need to
let . . . to let the whole house know you're here. Life's
difficult enough as it is. Have you got a match?
ALBERT: No, I . . . I don't think I have.
GIRL: Oh, God, you'd think you'd have a match.

He walks about.

I say, would you mind taking your shoes off? You're
really making a dreadful row. Really, I can't bear . . .
noisy . . . people.

*He looks at his shoes, begins to untie one. The GIRL searches
for matches on the mantelpiece, upon which are a number of
articles and objects, including a large alarm clock.*

I know I had one somewhere.
ALBERT: I've got a lighter.
GIRL: You can't light a gasfire with a lighter. You'd burn your
fingers.

She bends down to the hearth.

Where are the damn things? This is ridiculous. I die
without the fire. I simply die. [*She finds the box.*] Ah, here
we are. At last.

*She turns on the gas fire and lights it. He watches her. She
puts the matchbox on the mantelpiece and picks up a photo.*

Do you like this photo? It's of my little girl. She's staying
with friends. Rather fine, isn't she? Very aristocratic
features, don't you think? She's at a very select boarding
school at the moment, actually. In . . . Hereford, very
near Hereford. [*She puts the photo back.*] I shall be going
down for the prize day shortly. You do look idiotic standing
there with one shoe on and one shoe off. All lop-sided.

ALBERT pulls at the lace of his other shoe. The lace breaks. He swears shortly under his breath.

GIRL [*sharply*]: Do you mind not saying words like that?

ALBERT: I didn't . . .

GIRL: I heard you curse.

ALBERT: My lace broke.

GIRL: That's no excuse.

ALBERT: What did I say?

GIRL: I'm sorry, I can't bear that sort of thing. It's just . . . not in my personality.

ALBERT: I'm sorry.

GIRL: It's quite all right. It's just . . . something in my nature. I've got to think of my daughter, too, you know.

She crouches by the fire.

Come near the fire a minute. Sit down.

He goes towards a small stool.

Not on that! That's my seat. It's my own stool. I did the needlework myself. A long time ago.

He sits in a chair, opposite.

Which do you prefer, electric or gas? For a fire, I mean?

ALBERT [*holding his forehead, muttering*]: I don't know.

GIRL: There's no need to be rude, it was a civil question. I prefer gas. Or a log fire, of course. They have them in Switzerland.

[*Pause.*]

Have you got a headache?

ALBERT: No.

GIRL: I didn't realize you had a lighter. You don't happen to have any cigarettes on you, I suppose?

ALBERT: No.

GIRL: I'm very fond of a smoke. After dinner. With a glass of wine. Or before dinner, with sherry.

She stands and taps the mantelpiece, her eyes roaming over it.

You look as if you've had a night out. Where have you
been? Had a nice time?

ALBERT: Quite . . . quite nice.

GIRL [*sitting on the stool*]: What do you do?

ALBERT: I . . . work in films.

GIRL: Films? Really? What do you do?

ALBERT: I'm an assistant director.

GIRL: Really? How funny. I used to be a continuity girl. But
I gave it up.

ALBERT [*tonelessly*]: What a pity.

GIRL: Yes, I'm beginning to think you're right. You meet
such a good class of people. Of course, now you say you're
an assistant director I can see what you mean. I mean, I
could tell you had breeding the moment I saw you. You
looked a bit washed out, perhaps, but there was no mis-
taking the fact that you had breeding. I'm extremely particular, you see. I do like a certain amount of delicacy in
men . . . a certain amount . . . a certain degree . . .
a certain amount of refinement. You do see my point?
Some men I couldn't possibly entertain. Not even if I was
. . . starving. I don't want to be personal, but that word
you used, when you broke your lace, it made me shiver,
I'm just not that type, made me wonder if you were as
well bred as I thought . . .

He wipes his face with his hand.

You do look hot. Why are you so hot? It's chilly. Yes,
you remind me . . . I saw the most ghastly horrible fight
before, there was a man, one man, he was sweating . . .
sweating. You haven't been in a fight, by any chance? I
don't know how men can be so bestial. It's hardly much
fun for women, I can tell you. I don't want someone else's
blood on my carpet.

ALBERT *chuckles*.

What are you laughing at?
ALBERT: Nothing.
GIRL: It's not in the least funny.

ALBERT *looks up at the mantelpiece. His gaze rests there.*

What are you looking at?
ALBERT [*ruminatively*]: That's a nice big clock.

It is twenty past two.

GIRL [*with fatigue*]: Yes, it's late, I suppose we might as well
. . . Haven't you got a cigarette?
ALBERT: No.
GIRL [*jumping up*]: I'm sure I have, somewhere. [*She goes to
the table.*] Yes, here we are, I knew I had. I have to hide
them. The woman who comes in to do my room, she's very
light-fingered. I don't know why she comes in at all. Nobody wants her, all she does is spy on me, but I'm obliged
to put up with her, this room is serviced. Which means
I have to pay a pretty penny.

She lights her cigarette.

It's a dreadful area, too. I'm thinking of moving. The
neighbourhood is full of people of no class at all. I just don't
fit in.
ALBERT: Is that clock right?
GIRL: People have told me, the most distinguished people,
that I could go anywhere. You could go anywhere, they've
told me, you could be anything. I'm quite well educated,
you know. My father was a . . . he was a military man.
In the Army. Actually it was a relief to speak to you. I
haven't . . . spoken to anyone for some hours.

ALBERT *suddenly coughs violently.*

Oh, please don't do that! Use your handkerchief!

He sighs, and groans.

What on earth's the matter with you? What have you been doing tonight?

He looks at her and smiles.

ALBERT: Nothing.
GIRL: Really?

She belches.

Oh, excuse me. I haven't eaten all day. I had a tooth out. Hiccoughs come from not eating, don't they? Do you . . . do you want one of these?

She throws him a cigarette, which he slowly lights.

I mean, I'm no different from any other girl. In fact, I'm better. These so-called respectable girls, for instance, I'm sure they're much worse than I am. Well, you're an assistant director—all your continuity girls and secretaries, I'll bet they're . . . very loose.

ALBERT: Uh.
GIRL: Do you know what I've actually heard? I've heard that respectable married women, solicitors' wives, go out and pick men up when their husbands are out on business! Isn't that fantastic? I mean, they're supposed to be . . . they're supposed to be respectable!

ALBERT [*muttering*]: Fantastic.
GIRL: I beg your pardon?
ALBERT: I said it was fantastic.
GIRL: It is. You're right. Quite fantastic. Here's one thing, though. There's one thing that's always fascinated me. How far do men's girl friends go? I've often wondered.
   [*Pause.*]
   Eh?
ALBERT: Depends.

GIRL: Yes, I suppose it must.

[*Pause.*]

You mean on the girl?

ALBERT: What?

GIRL: You mean it depends on the girl?

ALBERT: It would do, yes.

GIRL: Quite possibly. I must admit that with your continuity girls and secretaries, I don't see why you . . . had to approach me. . . . Have you been on the town tonight, then? With a continuity girl?

ALBERT: You're a bit . . . worried about continuity girls, aren't you?

GIRL: Only because I've been one myself. I know what they're like. No better than they should be.

ALBERT: When were you a . . .?

GIRL: Years ago! [*Standing.*] You're nosey, aren't you?

She goes to the window.

Sometimes I wish the night would never end. I like sleeping. I could sleep . . . on and on.

ALBERT *stands and picks up the clock.*

Yes, you can see the station from here. All the trains go out, right through the night.

He stares at the clock.

I suppose we might as well . . . [*She turns and sees him.*] What are you doing? [*She crosses to him.*] What are you doing with that clock?

He looks at her, slowly.

Mmnn?

ALBERT: Admiring it.

GIRL: It's a perfectly ordinary clock. Give me it. I've seen too many people slip things into their pockets before now, as soon as your back's turned. Nothing personal, of course. [*She puts it back.*] Mind your ash! Don't spill it all over the floor! I have to keep this carpet immaculate. Otherwise the charlady, she's always looking for excuses for telling tales. Here. Here's an ashtray. Use it, please.

She gives it to him. He stares at her.

Sit down. Sit down. Don't stand about like that. What are you staring at me for?

He sits. She studies him.

Where's your wife?

ALBERT: Nowhere.

She stubs her cigarette.

GIRL: And what film are you making at the moment?

ALBERT: I'm on holiday.

GIRL: Where do you work?

ALBERT: I'm a free lance.

GIRL: You're . . . rather young to be in such a . . . high position, aren't you?

ALBERT: Oh?

GIRL [*laughs*]: You amuse me. You interest me. I'm a bit of a psychologist, you know. You're very young to be—what you said you were. There's something childish in your face, almost retarded. [*She laughs.*] I do like that word. I'm not being personal, of course . . . just being . . . psychological. Of course, I can see you're one for the girls. Don't know why you had to pick on me, at this time of night, really rather forward of you. I'm a respectable mother, you know, with a child at boarding school. You couldn't call me . . . anything else. All I do, I just entertain a few gentlemen, of my own choice, now and again. What girl doesn't?

His hand screws the cigarette. He lets it fall on the carpet.

[*Outraged.*] What do you think you're doing?

She stares at him.

Pick it up! Pick that up, I tell you! It's my carpet!

She lunges towards it.

It's not my carpet, they'll make me pay—

His hand closes upon hers as she reaches for it.

What are you doing? Let go. Treating my place like a pigsty. [*She looks up at him as he bends over her.*] Let me go. You're burning my carpet!

ALBERT [*quietly, intensely*]: Sit down.

GIRL: How dare you?

ALBERT: Shut up. Sit down.

GIRL [*struggling*]: What are you doing?

ALBERT [*erratically, trembling, but with quiet command*]: Don't scream. I'm warning you.

He lifts her by her wrist and presses her down on to the stool.

No screaming. I warn you.

GIRL: What's the—?

ALBERT [*through his teeth*]: Be quiet. I told you to be quiet. Now you be quiet.

GIRL: What are you going to do?

ALBERT [*seizing the clock from the mantelpiece*]: DON'T MUCK ME ABOUT!

She freezes with terror.

See this? One crack with this . . . just one crack . . . [*Viciously.*] Who do you think you are? You talk too much, you know that. You never stop talking. Just because you're a woman you think you can get away with it. [*Bending over her.*] You've made a mistake, this time. You've picked the wrong man.

He begins to grow in stature and excitement, passing the clock from hand to hand.

You're all the same, you see, you're all the same, you're just a dead weight round my neck. What makes you think . . . [*He begins to move about the room, at one point half crouching, at another standing upright, as if exercising his body.*] . . . What makes you think you can . . . tell me . . . yes . . . It's the same as this business about the light in Grandma's room. Always something. Always something. [*To her.*] My ash? I'll put it where I like! You see this clock? Watch your step. Just watch your step.

GIRL: Stop this. What are you—?

ALBERT [*seizing her wrist, with trembling, controlled violence*]: Watch your step! [*Stammering.*] I've had—I've had— I've had—just about enough. Get it? . . . You know what I did?

He looks at her and chuckles.

Don't be so frightened.

GIRL: I . . .

ALBERT [*casually*]: Don't be so frightened.

He squats by her, still holding the clock.

I'm just telling you. I'm just telling you, that's all. [*Breathlessly.*] You haven't got any breeding. She hadn't either. And what about those girls tonight? Same kind. And that one. I didn't touch her!

GIRL [*almost inaudible*]: What you been doing?

ALBERT: I've got as many qualifications as the next man. Let's get that quite . . . straight. And I got the answer to her. I got the answer to her, you see, tonight. . . . I finished the conversation . . . I finished it . . . I finished her . . .

She squirms. He raises the clock.

With this clock! [*Trembling.*] One . . . crack . . . with

. . . this. . . clock . . . finished! [*Thoughtfully.*] Of course,
I loved her, really. [*He suddenly sees the photograph on
the mantelpiece, puts the clock down and takes it. The* GIRL
*half rises and gasps, watching him. He looks at the photo
curiously.*] Uhhh? . . . Your daughter? . . . This a photo
of your daughter? . . . Uuuh? [*He breaks the frame and
takes out the photo.*]

GIRL [*rushes at him*]. Leave that!

ALBERT [*dropping the frame and holding the photo*]: Is it?

The GIRL *grabs at it.* ALBERT *clutches her wrist. He holds
her at arm's length.*

GIRL: Leave that! [*Writhing.*] What? Don't—it's mine!

ALBERT [*turns the photo over and reads back*]: 'Class Three
   Classical, Third Prize, Bronze Medal, Twickenham Com-
   petition, nineteen thirty-three.' [*He stares at her. The* GIRL
   stands, shivering and whimpering.] You liar. That's you.

GIRL: It's not!

ALBERT: That's not your daughter. It's you! You're just a
   fake, you're just all lies!

GIRL: Scum! Filthy scum!

ALBERT, *twisting her wrist, moves suddenly to her. The* GIRL
cringing, falls back into her chair.

ALBERT [*warningly*]: Mind how you talk to me. [*He crumples
   the photo.*]

GIRL [*moans*]: My daughter. My little girl. My little baby girl.

ALBERT: Get up.

GIRL: No . . .

ALBERT: Get up! Up!

She stands.

Walk over there, to the wall. Go on! Get over there. Do as
you're told. Do as I'm telling you. I'm giving the orders
here.

She walks to the wall.

Stop!

GIRL [*whimpering*]: What . . . do you want me to do?

ALBERT: Just keep your big mouth closed, for a start.

He frowns uncertainly.

Cover your face!

She does so. He looks about, blinking.

Yes. That's right. [*He sees his shoes.*] Come on, come on, pick up those shoes. Those shoes! Pick them up!

She looks for the shoes and picks them up.

That's right. [*He sits.*] Bring them over here. Come on. That's right. Put them on.

He extends his foot.

GIRL: You're . . .

ALBERT: On! Right on. That's it. That's it. That's more like it. That's . . . more like it! Good. Lace them! Good.

He stands. She crouches.

Silence.

He shivers and murmurs with the cold. He looks about the room.

ALBERT: It's cold.

[*Pause.*]

Ooh, it's freezing.

GIRL [*whispering*]: The fire's gone.

ALBERT [*looking at the window*]: What's that? Looks like light. Ooh, it's perishing. [*Looks about, muttering.*] What a dump. Not staying here. Getting out of this place.

He shivers and drops the clock. He looks down at it. She too. He kicks it across the room.

[*With a smile, softly.*] So you . . . bear that in mind. Mind how you talk to me.

He goes to door, then turns.

[*Flipping half a crown to her.*] Buy yourself a seat . . . buy yourself a seat at a circus.

He opens the door and goes.

SCENE THREE

The house.
The front door opens. ALBERT *comes in, a slight smile on his face. He saunters across the hall into the kitchen, takes off his jacket and throws it across the room. The same with his tie. He sits heavily, loosely, in a chair, his legs stretched out. Stretching his arms, he yawns luxuriously, scratches his head with both hands and stares ruminatively at the ceiling, a smile on his face. His mother's voice calls his name.*

MOTHER [*from the stairs*]: Albert!

His body freezes. His gaze comes down. His legs slowly come together. He looks in front of him.
His MOTHER *comes into the room, in her dressing gown. She stands, looking at him.*

Do you know what the time is?
[*Pause.*]
Where have you been?
[*Pause.*]
[*Reproachfully, near to tears.*] I don't know what to say to you, Albert. To raise your hand to your own mother. You've never done that before in your life. To threaten your own mother.
[*Pause.*]

That clock would have hurt me, Albert. And you'd have
been . . . I know you'd have been very sorry. Aren't I a
good mother to you? Everything I do is . . . is for your
own good. You should know that. You're all I've got.

*She looks at his slumped figure. Her reproach turns to solici-
tude.*

[*Gently.*] Look at you. You look washed out. Oh, you look
. . . I don't understand what could have come over you.

She takes a chair and sits close to him.

Listen, Albert, I'll tell you what I'm going to do. I'm going
to forget it. You see? I'm going to forget all about it.
We'll have your holiday in a fortnight. We can go away.

She strokes his hand.

We'll go away . . . together.
[*Pause.*]
It's not as if you're a bad boy . . . you're a good boy . . .
I know you are . . . it's not as if you're really bad, Albert,
you're not . . . you're not bad, you're good . . . you're
not a bad boy, Albert, I know you're not . . .
[*Pause.*]
You're good, you're not bad, you're a good boy . . . I
know you are . . . you are, aren't you?

The Dwarfs

The Dwarfs was first performed on the B.B.C. Third Programme on 2 December, 1960 with the following cast:-

LEN   Richard Pasco
PETE   Jon Rollason
MARK   Alex Scott

Produced by Barbara Bray

The play was first presented in a new version for the stage by Michael Codron and David Hall at the New Arts Theatre, London, on 18 September, 1963 with the following cast:-

LEN   John Hurt
PETE   Philip Bond
MARK   Michael Forrest

Directed by Harold Pinter
assisted by Guy Vaesen

The Dwarfs

The two main areas are:

1. *a room in* LEN'S *house. Solid middle-European furniture.*
Piles of books. A small carved table with a chenille cloth, a bowl
of fruit, books. Two marquetry chairs. A hanging lamp with
dark shade.

2. *the living room in* MARK'S *flat. Quite modern. Comfor-*
table. Two armchairs and a coffee table.

There is also a central downstage area of isolation and, for a
short scene later in the play, a bed in a hospital, upstage on a
higher level.

LEN, PETE *and* MARK *are all in their late twenties.*

MARK'S *room, midnight. Lamps are alight. Two cups and*
saucers, a sugar-bowl and a teapot are on a tray on the coffee table.

PETE *is sitting, reading.*

LEN *is playing a recorder. The sound is fragmentary.*

LEN: Pete.
PETE: What?
LEN: Come here.
PETE: What?
LEN: What's the matter with this recorder? [*He pulls recorder*
   in half, looks down, blows, taps.] There's something wrong
   with this recorder.
PETE: Let's have some tea.

LEN: I can't do a thing with it.

[*Re-assembles recorder. Another attempt to play.*]

Where's the milk?

[*He puts recorder on tray.*]

PETE: You were going to bring it.

LEN: That's right.

PETE: Well, where is it?

LEN: I forgot it. Why didn't you remind me?

PETE: Give me the cup.

LEN: What do we do now?

PETE: Give me the tea.

LEN: Without milk?

PETE: There isn't any milk.

LEN: What about sugar? [*Moving towards door.*] He must have a pint of milk somewhere. [*He exits to kitchen. Noise of opening cupboards etc. He reappears with a couple of gherkins in a jar.*] Here's a couple of gherkins. What about a gherkin? [*Takes jar to* PETE.] Fancy a gherkin. [PETE *sniffs, looks up in disgust.* LEN *sniffs and exits.*] Wait a minute. [*Kitchen noises.* LEN *reappears with a bottle of milk.*] Ah! Here we are. I knew he'd have a pint laid on. [*Pressing the top.*] Uuh! Uuuhh . . . . It's stiff.

PETE: I wouldn't open that.

LEN: Uuuhh . . . . why not? I can't drink tea without milk. Uuh! That's it. [*Picking up cup to pour.*] Give us your cup.

PETE: Leave it alone.

[*Pause.* LEN *shakes bottle over cup.*]

LEN: It won't come out. [*Pause.*] The milk won't come out of the bottle.

PETE: It's been in there two weeks, why should it come out?

LEN: Two weeks? He's been away longer than two weeks. [*Slight pause.*] It's stuck in the bottle. [*Slight pause.*] You'd think a man like him would have a maid, wouldn't you, to look after the place while he's away, to look after his milk? Or a gentleman. A gentleman's gentleman. Are you quite sure he hasn't got a gentleman's gentleman tucked away somewhere, to look after the place for him?

PETE [*rising to replace book on shelf*]: Only you. You're the only gentleman's gentleman he's got.

[*Pause.*]

LEN: Well, if I'm his gentleman's gentleman, I should have been looking after the place for him.

[*Pause.* PETE *takes brass toasting fork off wall.*]

PETE: What's this?

LEN: That? You've seen that before. It's a toasting fork.

PETE: It's got a monkey's head.

LEN: It's Portuguese. Everything in this house is Portuguese.

PETE: Why's that?

LEN: That's where he comes from.

PETE: Does he?

LEN: Or at least, his grandmother on his father's side. That's where the family comes from.

PETE: Well, well.

[*He hangs up the toasting fork.*]

LEN: What time's he coming?

PETE: Soon.

[*He pours himself a cup of tea.*]

LEN: You're drinking black tea.

PETE: What about it?

LEN: You're not in Poland.

[*He plays recorder.* PETE *sits in armchair.*]

PETE: What's the matter with that thing?

LEN: Nothing. There's nothing wrong with it. But it must be

broken. It's a year since I played it. [*He sneezes.*] Aah! I've got the most shocking blasted cold I've ever had in all my life. [*He blows his nose.*] Still, it's not much of a nuisance really.

PETE: Don't wear me out. [*Slight pause.*] Why don't you pull yourself together? You'll be ready for the loony bin next week if you go on like this.

[LEN *uses recorder as a telescope to the back of* PETE'S *head.*]

[*Pause.*]

LEN: Ten to one he'll be hungry.

PETE: Who?

LEN: Mark. When he comes. He can eat like a bullock, that bloke. Still, he won't find much to come home to, will he? There's nothing in the kitchen, there's not even a bit of lettuce. It's like the workhouse here. [*Pause.*] He can eat like a bullock, that bloke. [*Pause.*] I've seen him finish off a loaf of bread before I'd got my jacket off. [*Pause.*] He'd never leave a breadcrumb on a plate in the old days. [*Pause.*] Of course, he may have changed. Things do change. But I'm the same. Do you know, I had five solid square meals one day last week? At eleven o'clock, two o'clock, six o'clock, ten o'clock and one o'clock. Not bad going. Work makes me hungry. I was working that day. [*Pause.*] I'm always starving when I get up. Daylight has a funny effect on me. As for the night, that goes without saying. As far as I'm concerned the only thing you can do in the night is eat. It keeps me fit, especially if I'm at home. I have to run downstairs to put the kettle on, run upstairs to finish what I'm doing, run downstairs to cut a sandwich or arrange a salad, run upstairs to finish what I'm doing, run back downstairs to see to the sausages, if I'm having sausages, run back upstairs to finish what I'm doing, run back downstairs to lay the table, run back upstairs to finish what I'm doing, run back—

PETE: Yes!

LEN: Where did you get those shoes?

PETE: What?

LEN: Those shoes. How long have you had them?

PETE: What's the matter with them?

LEN: Have you been wearing them all night?

[*Pause.*]

PETE: When did you last sleep?

[*His hand is lying open, palm upward.*]

LEN: Sleep? Don't make me laugh. All I do is sleep.

PETE: What about work? How's work?

LEN: Paddington? It's a big railway station. An oven. It's an oven. Still, bad air is better than no air. It's best on night shift. The trains come in, I give a bloke half a dollar, he does my job, I curl up in the corner and read the timetables. But they tell me I might make a first class porter. I've been told I've got the makings of a number one porter. What are you doing with your hand?

PETE: What are you talking about?

LEN: What are you doing with your hand?

PETE [*coolly*]: What do you think I'm doing with it? Eh? What do you think?

LEN: I don't know.

PETE: I'll tell you, shall I? Nothing. I'm not doing anything with it. It's not moving. I'm doing *nothing* with it.

LEN: You're holding it palm upwards.

PETE: What about it?

LEN: It's not normal. Let's have a look at that hand. Let's have a look at it. [*Pause. He gasps through his teeth.*] You're a homicidal maniac.

PETE: Is that a fact?

LEN: Look. Look at that hand. Look, look at it. A straight line

right across the middle. Right across the middle, see?
Horizontal. That's all you've got. What else have you got?
You're a nut.

PETE: Oh yes?

LEN: You couldn't find two men in a million with a hand like
that. It sticks out a mile. A mile. That's what you are,
that's exactly what you are, you're a homicidal maniac!

[*A knock on the outer door.*]

PETE [*rising to exit*]: That's him. [*He goes off. The lights begin
to fade to blackout.*]

MARK: [*off*] Anyone here?

PETE: [*off*] Yes, how are you?

MARK: [*off*] Any tea?

PETE: [*off*] Polish tea.

[*Blackout. The lights come up in* LEN'S *room—overhead lamp.*

LEN *is sitting at the side of the table.*]

LEN: There is my table. That is a table. There is my chair.
There is my table. That is a bowl of fruit. There is my chair.
There are my curtains. There is no wind. It is past night
and before morning. This is my room. This is a room.
There is the wall-paper, on the walls. There are six walls.
Eight walls. An octagon. This room is an octagon.

There are my shoes, on my feet.

This is a journey and an ambush. This is the centre of the
cold, a halt to the journey and no ambush. This is the deep
grass I keep to. This is the thicket in the centre of the night
and the morning. There is my hundred watt bulb like a
dagger. This room moves. This room is moving. It has
moved. It has reached . . . a dead halt. This is my fixture.
There is no web. All's clear, and abundant. Perhaps a
morning will arrive. If a morning arrives, it will not destroy
my fixture, nor my luxury. If it is dark in the night or light,

nothing obtrudes. I have my compartment. I am wedged. Here is my arrangement, and my kingdom. There are no voices. They make no hole in my side.

The doorbell rings. LEN *searches for his glasses on the table, rummaging among the books. Lifts tablecloth. Is still. Searches in armchair. Then on mantlepiece. Bell rings again. He searches under table. Bell rings again. He rises, looks down, sees glasses in top pocket of jacket. Smiles, puts them on. Exits to open front door.* MARK *enters to below table.* LEN *follows.*

LEN: What's this, a suit? Where's your carnation?

MARK: What do you think of it?

LEN: It's not a schmutta.

MARK: It's got a zip at the hips.

LEN: A zip at the hips? What for?

MARK: Instead of a buckle. It's neat.

LEN: Neat? I should say it's neat.

MARK: No turn-ups.

LEN: I can see that. Why didn't you have turn-ups?

MARK: It's smarter without turn-ups.

LEN: Of course it's smarter without turn-ups.

MARK: I didn't want it double-breasted.

LEN: Double-breasted? Of course you couldn't have it double-breasted.

MARK: What do you think of the cloth?

LEN: The cloth? [*He examines it, gasps and whistles through his teeth. At a great pace.*] What a piece of cloth. What a piece of cloth. What a piece of cloth. What a piece of cloth. What a piece of *cloth*.

MARK: You like the cloth?

LEN: WHAT A PIECE OF CLOTH!

MARK: What do you think of the cut?

LEN: What do I think of the cut? The cut? The cut? What a cut!

What a cut! I've never seen such a cut! [*Pause.*] [*He sits and groans.*]

MARK [*combing his hair and sitting*]: Do you know where I've just been?

LEN: Where?

MARK: Earls Court.

LEN: Uuuuhh! What were you doing there? That's beside the point.

MARK: What's the matter with Earl's Court?

LEN: It's a mortuary without a corpse. [*Pause.*] There's a time and place for everything . . .

MARK: You're right there.

LEN: What do you mean by that?

MARK: There's a time and place for everything.

LEN: You're right there. [*Puts glasses on, rises to Mark.*] Who have you been with? Actors and actresses? What's it like when you act? Does it please you? Does it please anyone else?

MARK: What's wrong with acting?

LEN: It's a time-honoured profession—it's time-honoured. [*Pause.*] But what does it do? Does it please you when you walk onto a stage and everybody looks up and watches you? Maybe they don't want to watch you at all. Maybe they'd prefer to watch someone else. Have you ever asked them? [MARK *chuckles.*] You should follow my example and take up mathematics. [*Showing him open book.*] Look! All last night I was working at mechanics and determinants. There's nothing like a bit of calculus to cheer you up.

Pause.

MARK: I'll think about it.

LEN: Have you got a telephone here?

MARK: It's your house.

LEN: Yes. What are you doing here? What do you want here?

MARK: I thought you might give me some bread and honey.

LEN: I don't want you to become too curious in this room. There's no place for curiosities here. Keep a sense of proportion. That's all I ask.

MARK: That's all.

LEN: I've got enough on my plate with this room as it is.

MARK: What's the matter with it?

LEN: The rooms we live in . . . open and shut. [*Pause.*] Can't you see? They change shape at their own will. I wouldn't grumble if only they would keep to some consistency. But they don't. And I can't tell the limits, the boundaries, which I've been led to believe are natural. I'm all for the natural behaviour of rooms, doors, staircases, the lot. But I can't rely on them. When, for example, I look through a train window, at night, and see the yellow lights, very clearly, I can see what they are, and I see that they're still. But they're only still because I'm moving. I know that they do move along with me, and when we go round a bend, they bump off. But I know that they are still, just the same. They are, after all, stuck on poles which are rooted to the earth. So they must be still, in their own right, insofar as the earth itself is still, which of course it isn't. The point is, in a nutshell, that I can only appreciate such facts when I'm moving. When I'm still, nothing around me follows a natural course of conduct. I'm not saying I'm any criterion, I wouldn't say that. After all, when I'm on the train I'm not really moving at all. That's obvious. I'm in the corner seat. I'm still. I am perhaps being moved, but I do not move. Neither do the yellow lights. The train moves, granted, but what's a train got to do with it?

MARK: Nothing.

LEN: You're frightened.

MARK: Am I?

LEN: You're frightened that any moment I'm liable to put a red hot burning coal in your mouth.

MARK: Am I?

LEN: But when the time comes, you see, what I shall do is place the red hot burning coal in my own mouth.

Swift blackout. PETE *sits where* MARK *has been. Lights snap up.*

I've got some beigels.

PETE: This is a very solid table, isn't it?

LEN: I said I've got some biegels.

PETE: No thanks. How long have you had this table?

LEN: It's a family heirloom.

PETE: Yes, I'd like a good table, and a good chair. Solid stuff. Made for the bearer. I'd put them in a boat. Sail it down the river. A houseboat. You could sit in the cabin and look out at the water.

LEN: Who'd be steering?

PETE: You could park it. Park it. There's not a soul in sight.

LEN *brings half-full bottle of wine and glass to table. Reads label. Sniffs at bottle. Pours some into glass, savours then gargles, walking about. Spits wine back into glass, returns bottle and glass at sideboard, after a defensive glance at* PETE. *Returns to above table.*

LEN [*muttering*]: Impossible, impossible, impossible.

PETE [*briskly*]: I've been thinking about you.

LEN: Oh?

PETE: Do you know what your trouble is? You're not elastic. There's no elasticity in you. You want to be more elastic.

LEN: Elastic? Elastic. Yes, you're quite right. Elastic. What are you talking about?

PETE: Giving up the ghost isn't so much a failure as a tactical error. By elastic I mean being prepared for your own deviations. You don't know where you're going to come out next at the moment. You're like a rotten old shirt. Buck your ideas up. They'll lock you up before you're much older.

LEN: No. There is a different sky each time I look. The clouds run about in my eye. I can't do it.

PETE: The apprehension of experience must obviously be dependent upon discrimination if it's to be considered valuable. That's what you lack. You've got no idea how to preserve a distance between what you smell and what you think about it. You haven't got the faculty for making a simple distinction between one thing and another. Every time you walk out of this door you go straight over a cliff. What you've got to do is nourish the power of assessment. How can you hope to assess and verify anything if you walk about with your nose stuck between your feet all day long? You knock around with Mark too much. He can't do you any good. I know how to handle him. But I don't think he's your sort. Between you and me, I sometimes think he's a man of weeds. Sometimes I think he's just playing a game. But what game? I like him all right when you come down to it. We're old pals. But you look at him and what do you see? An attitude. Has it substance or is it barren? Sometimes I think it's as barren as a bombed site. He'll be a spent force in no time if he doesn't watch his step. [Pause.] I'll tell you a dream I had last night. I was with a girl in a tube station, on the platform. People were rushing about. There was some sort of panic. When I looked round I saw everyone's faces were peeling, blotched, blistered. People were screaming, booming down the tunnels. There was a fire bell clanging. When I looked at the girl I saw that her face was coming off in slabs too, like plaster. Black scabs and stains. The skin was dropping off like lumps of cat's meat. I could hear it sizzling on the eléctric rails. I pulled her by the arm to get her out of there.

She wouldn't budge. Stood there, with half a face, staring at me. I screamed at her to come away. Then I thought, Christ, what's my face like? Is that why she's staring? Is that rotting too?

Lights change. LEN'S *room.* PETE *and* MARK *looking at chess board.* LEN *watching them. Silence.*

LEN: Eh . . .

[*They don't look up.*]

The dwarfs are back on the job. [*Pause.*] I said the dwarfs are back on the job.

MARK: The what?

LEN: The dwarfs.

MARK: Oh yes?

LEN: Oh yes. They've been waiting for a smoke signal you see. I've just sent up the smoke signal.

[*Pause.*]

MARK: You've just sent it up, have you?

LEN: Yes. I've called them in on the job. They've taken up their positions. Haven't you noticed?

PETE: I haven't noticed. [*To* MARK.] Have you noticed?

MARK *chuckles.*

LEN: But I'll tell you one thing. They don't stop work until the job in hand is finished, one way or another. They never run out on a job. Oh no. They're true professionals. Real professionals.

PETE: Listen. Can't you see we're trying to play chess?

Pause.

LEN: I've called them in to keep an eye on you two, you see. They're going to keep a very close eye on you. So am I. We're waiting for you to show your hand. We're all going to keep a very close eye on you two. Me and the dwarfs.

Pause.

MARK: [*referring to chess*]: I think I've got you knackered, Pete.

PETE *looks at him.*

PETE: Do you?

Lights change and come up full in MARK'S *room.* LEN *enters with old gilt mirror.* MARK *follows.*

MARK: Put that mirror back.

LEN: This is the best piece of furniture you've got in the house. It's Spanish. No Portuguese. You're Portuguese, aren't you?

MARK: Put it back.

LEN: Look at your face in this mirror. Look. It's a farce. Where are your features? You haven't got any features. You couldn't call those features. What are you going to do about it, eh? What's the answer?

MARK: Mind that mirror. It's not insured.

LEN: I saw Pete the other day. In the evening. You didn't know that. I wonder about you. I often wonder about you. But I must keep pedalling. I must. There's a time limit. Who have you got hiding here? You're not alone here. What about your Esperanto? Don't forget, anything over two ounces goes up a penny.

MARK: Thanks for the tip.

LEN: Here's your mirror.

MARK exits with mirror. LEN *picks out apple from a fruit bowl, sits in armchair staring at it.* MARK *returns.*

This is a funny-looking apple.

[*He tosses it back to* MARK, *who replaces it.*]

Pete asked me to lend him a shilling.

MARK: Uh?

LEN: I refused.

MARK: What?

LEN: I refused downright to lend him a shilling.

MARK: What did he say to that?

LEN: Plenty. Since I left him I've been thinking thoughts I've never thought before. I've been thinking thoughts I've never thought before.

MARK: You spend too much time with Pete.

LEN: What?

MARK: Give it a rest. He doesn't do you any good. I'm the only one who knows how to get on with him. I can handle him. You can't. You take him too seriously. He doesn't worry me. I know how to handle him. He doesn't take any liberties with me.

LEN: Who says he takes liberties with me? Nobody takes liberties with me. I'm not the sort of man you can take liberties with.

MARK: You should drop it.

LEN *sees toasting fork, takes it to* MARK.

LEN: This is a funny toasting fork. Do you ever make any toast?

He drops the fork on the floor.

Don't touch it! You don't know what will happen if you touch it! You mustn't touch it! You mustn't bend! Wait. [*Pause.*] I'll bend. I'll . . . pick it up. I'm going to touch it. [*Pause . . . softly.*] There. You see? Nothing happens when I touch it. Nothing. Nothing can happen. No one would bother. [*A broken sigh.*] You see, I can't see the broken glass. I can't see the mirror I have to look through. I see the other side. The other side. But I can't see the mirror side. [*Pause.*] I want to break it, all of it. But how can I break it? How can I break it when I can't see it?

Lights fade and come up again in MARK'S *room.* LEN *is sitting in an arm chair.* MARK *enters with whisky bottle and two glasses. He pours drinks for* PETE *and himself.* PETE, *who has followed him in, takes his glass.* MARK *sits in other armchair. Neither take any notice of* LEN.

Silence.

PETE: Thinking got me into this and thinking's got to get me out. You know what I want? An efficient idea. You know what I mean? An efficient idea. One that'll work. Something I can pin my money on. An each way bet. Nothing's guaranteed, I know that. But I'm willing to gamble. I gambled when I went to work in the city. I want to fight them on their own ground, not moan about them from a distance. I did it and I'm still living. But I've had my fill of these city guttersnipes—all that scavenging scum! They're the sort of people, who, if the gates of heaven opened to them, all they'd feel would be a draught. I'm wasting away down there. The time has come to act. I'm after something truly workable, something deserving of the proper and active and voluntary application of my own powers. And I'll find it.

LEN: I squashed a tiny insect on a plate the other day. And I brushed the remains off my finger with my thumb. Then I saw that the fragments were growing, like fluff. As they were falling, they were becoming larger, like fluff. I had put my hand into the body of a dead bird.

PETE: The trouble is, you've got to be quite sure of what you mean by efficient. Look at a nutcracker. You press the cracker and the cracker cracks the nut. You might think that's an exact process. It's not. The nut cracks, but the hinge of the cracker gives out a friction which is completely incidental to the particular idea. It's unnecessary, an escape and wastage of energy to no purpose. So there's nothing efficient about a nutcracker. [*Pete sits, drinks*].

LEN: They've gone on a picnic.

MARK: Who?

LEN: The dwarfs.

PETE: Oh Christ. [*Picks up paper.*]

LEN: They've left me to sweep the yard, to keep the place in
order. It's a bloody liberty. They're supposed to be
keeping you under observation. What do they think I am,
a bloody charlady? I can't look after the place by myself,
it's not possible. Piles and piles and piles of muck and
leavings all over the place, spewed up spewed up, I'm not a
skivvy, they don't pay me, I pay them.

MARK: Why don't you settle down?

LEN: Oh don't worry, it's basically a happy relationship. I
trust them. They're very efficient. They know what they're
waiting for. But they've got a new game, did I tell you?
It's to do with beetles and twigs. There's a rockery of red-
hot cinder. I like watching them. Their hairs are curled
and oily on their necks. Always squatting and bending,
dipping their wicks in the custard. Now and again a lick
of flame screws up their noses. Do you know what they do?
They run wild. They yowl, they pinch, they dribble, they
whimper, they gouge, and then they soothe each others'
orifices with a local ointment, and then, all gone, all forgotten, they lark about, each with his buddy, get out the
nose spray and the scented syringe, settle down for the
night with a bun and a doughnut.

PETE: See you Mark. [*Exit.*]

MARK: Why don't you put it on the table? [*Pause.*] Open it
up, Len. [*Pause.*] I'm supposed to be a friend of yours.

LEN: You're a snake in my house.

MARK: Really?

LEN: You're trying to buy and sell me. You think I'm a ventriloquist's dummy. You've got me pinned to the wall before I open my mouth. You've got a tab on me, you're buying me out of house and home, you're a calculating bastard. [*Pause.*] Answer me. Say something. [*Pause.*] Do you understand? [*Pause.*] You don't agree? [*Pause.*] You disagree? [*Pause.*] You think I'm mistaken? [*Pause.*] But am I? [*Pause.*] Both of you bastards, you've made a hole in my side, I can't plug it! [*Pause.*] I've lost a kingdom. I suppose you're taking good care of things. Did you know that you and Pete are a music hall act? What happens? What do you do when you're alone? Do you do a jig? I suppose you're taking good care of things. I've got my treasure too. It's in my corner. Everything's in my corner. Everything is from the corner's point of view. I don't hold the whip. I'm a labouring man. I do the corner's will. I slave my guts out. I thought, at one time, that I'd escaped it, but it never dies, it's never dead. I feed it, it's well fed. Things that at one time seem to me of value I have no resource but to give it to eat and what was of value turns into pus. I can hide nothing. I can't lay anything aside. Nothing can be put aside, nothing can be hidden, nothing can be saved, it waits, it eats, it's voracious, you're in it, Pete's in it, you're all in my corner. There must be somewhere else!

Swift cross fade of lights to down centre area.

PETE *is seen vaguely, standing downstage below* LEN'S *room.* MARK *is seated in his room. Unlit.* LEN *crouches, watching* PETE.

Pete walks by the river. Under the woodyard wall stops. Stops. Hiss of the yellow grass. The wood battlements jaw over the wall. Dust in the fairground ticks. The night ticks.

He hears the tick of the roundabout, up river with the sweat. Pete walks by the river. Under the woodyard wall stops. Stops. The wood hangs. Deathmask on the water. Pete walks by the — gull. Slicing gull. Gull. Down. He stops. Rat corpse in the yellow grass. Gull pads. Gull probes. Gull stamps his feet. Gull whinnies up. Gull screams, tears, Pete, tears, digs, Pete cuts, breaks, Pete stretches the corpse, flaps his wings, Pete's beak grows, probes, digs, pulls, the river jolts, no moon, what can I see, the dwarfs collect, they slide down the bridge, they scutter by the shoreside, the dwarfs collect, capable, industrious, they wear raincoats, it is going to rain, Pete digs, he screws in to the head, the dwarfs watch, Pete tugs, he tugs, he's tugging, he kills, he's killing, the rat's head, with a snap the cloth of the rat's head tears. Pete walks by the . . . [*Deep groan.*]

He sinks into chair left of his table. Lights in LEN's *room swiftly fade up.* PETE *turns to him.*

PETE: You look the worse for wear. What's the matter with you?

LEN: I've been ill.

PETE: Ill? What's the matter?

LEN: Cheese. Stale cheese. It got me in the end. I've been eating a lot of cheese.

PETE: Yes, well, it's easy to eat too much cheese.

LEN: It all came out, in about twenty-eight goes. I couldn't stop shivering and I couldn't stop squatting. It got me all right. I'm all right now. I only go three times a day now. I can more or less regulate it. Once in the morning. A quick dash before lunch. Another quick dash after tea, and then I'm free to do what I want. I don't think you understand. That cheese didn't die. It only began to live when you swallowed it, you see, after it had gone down. I bumped into a German one night, he came home with me and helped me finish it off. He took it to bed with him, he sat up in bed with it, in the guest's suite. I went in and had a gander. He had it taped. He was brutal with it. He would bite into it and then concentrate. I had to hand it to him. The sweat came out on his nose but he stayed on his feet. After he'd got out of bed, that was. Stood bolt upright, swallowed it, clicked his fingers, ordered another piece of blackcurrant pie. It's my pie-making season. His piss stank worse than the cheese. You look in the pink.

PETE: You want to watch your step. You know that? You're going from bad to worse. Why don't you pull yourself together? Eh? Get a steady job. Cultivate a bit of go and guts for a change. Make yourself useful, mate, for Christ's sake. As you are, you're just a dead weight round everybody's neck. You want to listen to your friends, mate. Who else have you got?

PETE *taps him on the shoulder and exits. A light comes up on* MARK. *The lights in* LEN'S *room fade out.* LEN *rises to down centre.*

LEN: Mark sits by the fireside. Crosses his legs. His fingers wear a ring. The finger poised. Mark regards his finger. He regards his legs. He regards the fireside. Outside the door is the black blossom. He combs his hair with an ebony comb, he sits, he lies, he lowers his eyelashes, raises them, sees no change in the posture of the room, lights a cigarette, watches his hand clasp the lighter, watches the flame, sees his mouth go forward, sees the consummation, is satisfied. Pleased, sees the smoke in the lamp, pleased with the lamp and the smoke and his bulk, pleased with his legs and his ring and his hand and his body in the lamp. Sees himself speaking, the words arranged on his lips, sees himself with pleasure silent.
Under the twigs they slide, by the lilac bush, break the

stems, sit, scutter to the edge of the lawn and there wait, capable, industrious, put up their sunshades, watch. Mark lies, heavy, content, watches his smoke in the window, times his puff out, his hand fall, [*with growing disgust*] smiles at absent guests, sucks in all comers, arranges his web, lies there a spider.

LEN *moves to above armchair in* MARK'S *room as lights fade up. Down centre area fades out.*

What did you say?

MARK: I never said anything.

LEN: What do you do when you're tired, go to bed?

MARK: That's right.

LEN: You sleep like a log.

MARK: Yes.

LEN: What do you do when you wake up?

MARK: Wake up.

LEN: I want to ask you a question.

MARK: No doubt.

LEN: Are you prepared to answer questions?

MARK: No.

LEN: What do you do in the day when you're not walking about?

MARK: I rest.

LEN: Where do you find a resting place?

MARK: Here and there.

LEN: By consent?

MARK: Invariably.

LEN: But you're not particular?

MARK: Yes, I'm particular.

LEN: You choose your resting place?

MARK: Normally.

LEN: That might be anywhere?

MARK: Yes.

LEN: Does that content you?

MARK: Sure! I've got a home. I know where I live.

LEN: You mean you've got roots. Why haven't I got roots? My house is older than yours. My family lived here. Why haven't I got a home?

MARK: Move out.

LEN: Do you believe in God?

MARK: What?

LEN: Do you believe in God?

MARK: Who?

LEN: God.

MARK: God?

LEN: Do you believe in God?

MARK: Do I believe in God?

LEN: Yes.

MARK: Would you say that again?

LEN *goes swiftly to shelf. Picks up biscuit jar. Offers to* MARK.

LEN: Have a biscuit.

MARK: Thanks.

LEN: They're your biscuits.

MARK: There's two left. Have one yourself.

LEN *puts biscuits away.*

LEN: You don't understand. You'll never understand.

MARK: Really?

LEN: Do you know what the point is? Do you know what it is?

MARK: No.

LEN: The point is, who are you? Not why or how, not even what. I can see what, perhaps, clearly enough. But who are you? It's no use saying you know who you are just because you tell me you can fit your particular key into a particular slot, which will only receive your particular key because that's not foolproof and certainly not conclusive. Just because you're inclined to make these statements of faith has nothing to do with me. It's not my business. Occasionally I believe I perceive a little of what you are but that's pure accident. Pure accident on both our parts, the perceived and the perceiver. It's nothing like an accident, it's deliberate, it's a joint pretence. We depend on these accidents, on these contrived accidents, to continue. It's not important then that it's conspiracy or hallucination. What you are, or appear to be to me, or appear to be to you, changes so quickly, so horrifyingly, I certainly can't keep up with it and I'm damn sure you can't either. But who you are I can't even begin to recognize, and sometimes I recognize it so wholly, so forcibly, I can't look, and how can I be certain of what I see? You have no number. Where am I to look, where am I to look, what is there to locate, so as to have some surety, to have some rest from this whole bloody racket? You're the sum of so many reflections. How many reflections? Whose reflections? Is that what you consist of? What scum does the tide leave? What happens to the scum? When does it happen? I've seen what happens. But I can't speak when I see it. I can only point a finger. I can't even do that. The scum is broken and sucked back. I don't see where it goes. I don't see when, what do I see, what have I seen? What have I seen, the scum or the essence? What about it? Does all this give you the right to stand there and tell me you know who you are? It's a bloody impertinence. There's a great desert and there's a wind stopping. Pete's been eating too much cheese, he's ill from it, it's eating his flesh away, but that doesn't matter, you're still both in the same boat, you're eating all my biscuits, but that doesn't matter, you're still both in the same boat, you're still standing behind the curtains together. He thinks you're a fool, Pete thinks you're a fool, but that doesn't matter, you're still both of you standing behind my curtains, moving my curtains in my room. He may be your

Black Knight, you may be his Black Knight, but I'm cursed with the two of you, with two Black Knight's, that's friendship, that's this that I know. That's what I know.

MARK: Pete thinks I'm a fool? [*Pause.*] Pete . . . . Pete thinks that I'm a *fool*?

LEN *exits. Lights in* MARK'S *room fade out and then fade in again. Doorbell rings.* MARK *rises, goes off to front door.*

Silence.

PETE [*entering*]: Hullo, Mark.
MARK [*re-enters and sits again*]: Hullo.
PETE: What are you doing?
MARK: Nothing.
PETE: Can I sit down?
MARK: Sure.

Pete sits right armchair. Pause.

PETE: Well, what are you doing with yourself?
MARK: When's that?
PETE: Now.
MARK: Nothing.

MARK *files his nails.*

[*Pause.*]

PETE: Len's in hospital.
MARK: Len? What's the matter with him?
PETE: Kidney trouble. Not serious. [*Pause.*] Well, what have you been doing with yourself?
MARK: When?
PETE: Since I saw you.
MARK: This and that.
PETE: This and what?

MARK: That.

[*Pause.*]

PETE: Do you want to go and see Len?
MARK: When? Now?
PETE: Yes. It's visiting time. [*Pause.*] Are you busy?
MARK: No.

[*Pause.*]

PETE: What's up?
MARK: What?
PETE: What's up?
MARK: What do you mean?
PETE: You're wearing a gasmask.
MARK: Not me.

[*Pause.*]

PETE [*rising*]: Ready?
MARK: Yes. [*He rises and exits.*]
PETE [*as he follows* MARK *off*]: Fine day. [*Pause.*] Bit chilly.

The door slams as they leave the house. Lights up on LEN *in hospital bed. Listening to wireless (earphones).*

PETE *and* MARK *enter.*

LEN: You got here.
PETE [*sitting left of bed*]: Yes.
LEN: They can't do enough for me here.
PETE: Why's that?
LEN: Because I'm no trouble. [MARK *sits right of bed.*] They treat me like a king. These nurses, they treat me exactly like a king. [*Pause.*] Mark looks as though he's caught a crab.
MARK: Do I?
PETE: Airy, this ward.

LEN: Best quality blankets, home cooking, everything you could wish for. Look at the ceiling. It's not too high and it's not too low.

[*Pause.*]

PETE: By the way, Mark, what happened to your pipe?
MARK: Nothing happened to it.

[*Pause.*]

LEN: You smoking a pipe? [*Pause.*] What's it like out today?
PETE: Bit chilly.
LEN: Bound to be.
PETE: The sun's come out.
LEN: The sun's come out? [*Pause.*] Well, Mark, bring off the treble chance this week?
MARK: Not me.
    [*Pause.*]
LEN: Who's driving the tank?
PETE: What?
LEN: Who's driving the tank?
PETE: Don't ask me. We've been walking up the road back to back.
LEN: You've what? [*Pause.*] You've been walking up the road back to back? [*Pause.*] What are you doing sitting on my bed? You're not supposed to sit on the bed, you're supposed to sit on the chairs!
PETE [*rising and moving off*]: Well, give me a call when you get out. [*He exits.*]
MARK [*rising and following him*]: Yes give me a call. [*He exits.*]
LEN: [*calling after them*]: How do I know you'll be in?

Blackout. Lights come up on MARK'S *flat.* MARK *enters and sits.* PETE *enters, glances at* MARK, *sits.*

PETE: Horizontal personalities, those places. You're the only vertical. Makes you feel dizzy. [*Pause.*] You ever been inside one of those places?

MARK: I can't remember.

PETE: Right. [*Stubs out cigarette, rises, goes to exit.*]

MARK: All right. Why do you knock on my door?

PETE: What?

MARK: Come on. Why do you knock on my door?

PETE: What are you talking about?

MARK: Why?

PETE: I call to see you.

MARK: What do you want with me? Why come and see me?

PETE: Why?

MARK: You're playing a double game. You've been playing a double game. You've been using me. You've been leading me up the garden.

PETE: Mind how you go.

MARK: You've been wasting my time. For years.

PETE: Don't push me boy.

MARK: You think I'm a fool.

PETE: Is that what I think?

MARK: That's what you think. You think I'm a fool.

PETE: You are a fool.

MARK: You've always thought that.

PETE: From the beginning.

MARK: You've been leading me up the garden.

PETE: And you.

MARK: You know what you are? You're an infection.

PETE: Don't believe it. All I've got to do to destroy you is to leave you as you wish to be.

He walks out of the room. MARK *stares, slowly goes off as lights fade. Lights come up on down centre area. Enter* LEN.

LEN: They've stopped eating. It'll be a quick get out when the whistle blows. All their belongings are stacked in piles.

They've doused the fire. But I've heard nothing. What is the cause for alarm? Why is everything packed? Why are they ready for the off? But they say nothing. They've cut me off without a penny. And now they've settled down to a wide-eyed kip, crosslegged by the fire. It's insupportable. I'm left in the lurch. Not even a stale frankfurter, a slice of bacon rind, a leaf of cabbage, not even a mouldy piece of salami, like they used to sling me in the days when we told old tales by suntime. They sit, chock-full. But I smell a rat. They seem to be anticipating a rarer dish, a choicer spread. And this change. All about me the change. The yard as I know it is littered with scraps of cat's meat, pig bollocks, tin cans, bird brains, spare parts of all the little animals, a squelching, squealing carpet, all the dwarfs' leavings spittled in the muck, worms stuck in the poisoned shit heaps, the alleys a whirlpool of piss, slime, blood, and fruit juice. Now all is bare. All is clean. All is scrubbed. There is a lawn. There is a shrub. There is a flower.

Revue Sketches

Last to Go and *Request Stop* were performed in the revue *Pieces of Eight* at the Apollo Theatre, London, in 1959.

The Black and White and *Trouble in the Works* were performed in the revue *One to Another* at the Lyric Opera House, Hammersmith, and at the Apollo Theatre, London, in 1959.

TROUBLE IN THE WORKS

An office in a factory. MR. FIBBS *at the desk. A knock at the
door. Enter* MR. WILLS.

FIBBS: Ah, Wills. Good. Come in. Sit down, will you?
WILLS: Thanks, Mr. Fibbs.
FIBBS: You got my message?
WILLS: I just got it.
FIBBS: Good. Good.

Pause.

Good. Well now . . . Have a cigar?
WILLS: No, thanks, not for me, Mr. Fibbs.
FIBBS: Well, now, Wills, I hear there's been a little trouble
in the factory.
WILLS: Yes, I . . . I suppose you could call it that, Mr. Fibbs.
FIBBS: Well, what in heaven's name is it all about?
WILLS: Well, I don't exactly know how to put it, Mr. Fibbs.
FIBBS: Now come on, Wills, I've got to know what it is, before
I can do anything about it.
WILLS: Well, Mr. Fibbs, it's simply a matter that the men
have . . . well, they seem to have taken a turn against
some of the products.
FIBBS: Taken a turn?
WILLS: They just don't seem to like them much any more.
FIBBS: Don't like them? But we've got the reputation of
having the finest machine part turnover in the country.
They're the best paid men in the industry. We've got the
cheapest canteen in Yorkshire. No two menus are alike.
We've got a billiard hall, haven't we, on the premises, we've
got a swimming pool for use of staff. And what about the
long-playing record room? And you tell me they're dis-
satisfied?

WILLS: Oh, the men are very grateful for all the amenities, sir. They just don't like the products.

FIBBS: But they're beautiful products. I've been in the business a lifetime. I've never seen such beautiful products.

WILLS: There it is, sir.

FIBBS: Which ones don't they like?

WILLS: Well, there's the brass pet cock, for instance.

FIBBS: The brass pet cock? What's the matter with the brass pet cock?

WILLS: They just don't seem to like it any more.

FIBBS: But what exactly don't they like about it?

WILLS: Perhaps it's just the look of it.

FIBBS: That brass pet cock? But I tell you it's perfection. Nothing short of perfection.

WILLS: They've just gone right off it.

FIBBS: Well, I'm flabbergasted.

WILLS: It's not only the brass pet cock, Mr. Fibbs.

FIBBS: What else?

WILLS: There's the hemi unibal spherical rod end.

FIBBS: The hemi unibal spherical rod end? Where could you find a finer rod end?

WILLS: There are rod ends and rod ends, Mr. Fibbs.

FIBBS: I know there are rod ends and rod ends. But where could you find a finer hemi unibal spherical rod end?

WILLS: They just don't want to have anything more to do with it.

FIBBS: This is shattering. Shattering. What else? Come on, Wills. There's no point in hiding anything from me.

WILLS: Well, I hate to say it, but they've gone very vicious about the high speed taper shank spiral flute reamers.

FIBBS: The high speed taper shank spiral flute reamers! But that's absolutely ridiculous! What could they possibly have against the high speed taper shank spiral flute reamers?

WILLS: All I can say is they're in a state of very bad agitation about them. And then there's the gunmetal side outlet relief with handwheel.

FIBBS: What!

WILLS: There's the nippled connector and the nippled adaptor and the vertical mechanical comparator.

FIBBS: No!

WILLS: And the one they can't speak about without trembling is the jaw for Jacob's chuck for use on portable drill.

FIBBS: My own Jacob's chuck? Not my very own Jacob's chuck?

WILLS: They've just taken a turn against the whole lot of them, I tell you. Male elbow adaptors, tubing nuts, grub screws, internal fan washers, dog points, half dog points, white metal bushes—

FIBBS: But not, surely not, my lovely parallel male stud couplings.

WILLS: They hate and detest your lovely parallel male stud couplings, and the straight flange pump connectors, and back nuts, and front nuts, *and* the bronzedraw off cock with handwheel and the bronzedraw off cock without handwheel!

FIBBS: Not the bronzedraw off cock with handwheel?

WILLS: And without handwheel.

FIBBS: Without handwheel?

WILLS: And with handwheel.

FIBBS: Not with handwheel?

WILLS: And without handwheel.

FIBBS: Without handwheel?

WILLS: With handwheel *and* without handwheel.

FIBBS: With handwheel *and* without handwheel?

WILLS: With or without!

Pause.

FIBBS [*broken*]: Tell me. What do they want to make in its place?

WILLS: Brandy balls.

THE BLACK AND WHITE

The FIRST OLD WOMAN *is sitting at a milk bar table. Small.*
A SECOND OLD WOMAN *approaches. Tall. She is carrying two*
  bowls of soup, which are covered by two plates, on each of
  which is a slice of bread. She puts the bowls down on the
  table carefully.

SECOND: You see that one come up and speak to me at the
  counter?

  She takes the bread plates off the bowls, takes two spoons
  from her pocket, and places the bowls, plates and spoons.

FIRST: You got the bread, then?
SECOND: I didn't know how I was going to carry it. In the end
  I put the plates on top of the soup.
FIRST: I like a bit of bread with my soup.

  They begin the soup. Pause.

SECOND: Did you see that one come up and speak to me at
  the counter?
FIRST: Who?
SECOND: Comes up to me, he says, hullo, he says, what's the
  time by your clock? Bloody liberty. I was just standing
  there getting your soup.
FIRST: It's tomato soup.
SECOND: What's the time by your clock? he says.
FIRST: I bet you answered him back.
SECOND: I told him all right. Go on, I said, why don't you
  get back into your scraghole, I said, clear off out of it before
  I call a copper.

  Pause.

FIRST: I not long got here.

SECOND: Did you get the all-night bus?

FIRST: I got the all-night bus straight here.

SECOND: Where from?

FIRST: Marble Arch.

SECOND: Which one?

FIRST: The two-nine-four, that takes me all the way to Fleet Street.

SECOND: So does the two-nine-one. [*Pause.*] I see you talking to two strangers as I come in. You want to stop talking to strangers, old piece of boot like you, you mind who you talk to.

FIRST: I wasn't talking to any strangers.

Pause. The FIRST OLD WOMAN *follows the progress of a bus through the window.*

That's another all-night bus gone down. [*Pause.*] Going up the other way. Fulham way. [*Pause.*] That was a two-nine-seven. [*Pause.*] I've never been up that way. [*Pause.*] I've been down to Liverpool Street.

SECOND: That's up the other way.

FIRST: I don't fancy going down there, down Fulham way, and all up there.

SECOND: Uh-uh.

FIRST: I've never fancied that direction much.

Pause.

SECOND: How's your bread?

Pause.

FIRST: Eh?

SECOND: Your bread.

FIRST: All right. How's yours?

Pause.

SECOND: They don't charge for the bread if you have soup.

FIRST: They do if you have tea.

SECOND: If you have tea they do. [*Pause.*] You talk to strangers they'll take you in. Mind my word. Coppers'll take you in.

FIRST: I don't talk to strangers.

SECOND: They took me away in the wagon once.

FIRST: They didn't keep you though.

SECOND: They didn't keep me, but that was only because they took a fancy to me. They took a fancy to me when they got me in the wagon.

FIRST: Do you think they'd take a fancy to me?

SECOND: I wouldn't back on it.

The FIRST OLD WOMAN *gazes out of the window.*

FIRST: You can see what goes on from this top table. [*Pause.*] It's better than going down to that place on the embankment, anyway.

SECOND: Yes, there's not too much noise.

FIRST: There's always a bit of noise.

SECOND: Yes, there's always a bit of life.

Pause.

FIRST: They'll be closing down soon to give it a scrub-round.

SECOND: There's a wind out.

Pause.

FIRST: I wouldn't mind staying.

SECOND: They won't let you.

FIRST: I know. [*Pause.*] Still, they only close hour and half, don't they? [*Pause.*] It's not long. [*Pause.*] You can go along, then come back.

SECOND: I'm going. I'm not coming back.

FIRST: When it's light I come back. Have my tea.

SECOND: I'm going. I'm going up to the Garden.

FIRST: I'm not going down there. [*Pause.*] I'm going up to Waterloo Bridge.

SECOND: You'll just about see the last two-nine-six come up over the river.

FIRST: I'll just catch a look of it. Time I get up there.

Pause.

It don't look like an all-night bus in daylight, do it?

REQUEST STOP

A queue at a Request Bus Stop. A WOMAN *at the head, with a* SMALL MAN *in a raincoat next to her, two other* WOMEN *and a* MAN.

WOMAN [*to* SMALL MAN]: I beg your pardon, what did you say?

Pause.

All I asked you was if I could get a bus from here to Shepherds Bush.

Pause.

Nobody asked you to start making insinuations.

Pause.

Who do you think you are?

Pause.

Huh. I know your sort, I know your type. Don't worry, I know all about people like you.

Pause.

We can all tell where you come from. They're putting your sort inside every day of the week.

Pause.

All I've got to do, is report you, and you'd be standing in the dock in next to no time. One of my best friends is a plain clothes detective.

Pause.

I know all about it. Standing there as if butter wouldn't melt in your mouth. Meet you in a dark alley it'd be . . . another story. [*To the others, who stare into space.*] You heard what this man said to me. All I asked him was if I could get a bus from here to Shepherds Bush. [*To him.*] I've got witnesses, don't you worry about that.

Pause.

Impertinence.

Pause.

Ask a man a civil question he treats you like a threepenny bit. [*To him.*] I've got better things to do, my lad, I can assure you. I'm not going to stand here and be insulted on a public highway. Anyone can tell you're a foreigner. I was born just around the corner. Anyone can tell you're just up from the country for a bit of a lark. I know your sort.

Pause.

She goes to a LADY.

Excuse me lady. I'm thinking of taking this man up to the magistrate's court, you heard him make that crack, would you like to be a witness?

The LADY *steps into the road.*

LADY: Taxi . . .

She disappears.

WOMAN: We know what sort she is. [*Back to position.*] I was the first in this queue.

Pause.

Born just round the corner. Born and bred. These people from the country haven't the faintest idea of how to behave. Peruvians. You're bloody lucky I don't put you on a charge. You ask a straightforward question—

The others suddenly thrust out their arms at a passing bus. They run off left after it. The WOMAN, *alone, clicks her teeth and mutters. A man walks from the right to the stop, and waits. She looks at him out of the corner of her eye. At length she speaks shyly, hesitantly, with a slight smile.*

Excuse me. Do you know if I can get a bus from here . . . to Marble Arch?

LAST TO GO

A coffee stall. A BARMAN *and an old* NEWSPAPER SELLER. *The* BARMAN *leans on his counter, the* OLD MAN *stands with tea. Silence.*

MAN: You was a bit busier earlier.
BARMAN: Ah.
MAN: Round about ten.
BARMAN: Ten, was it?
MAN: About then.

Pause.

I passed by here about then.
BARMAN: Oh yes?
MAN: I noticed you were doing a bit of trade.

Pause.

BARMAN: Yes, trade was very brisk here about ten.
MAN: Yes, I noticed.

Pause.

I sold my last one about then. Yes. About nine forty-five.
BARMAN: Sold your last then, did you?
MAN: Yes, my last 'Evening News' it was. Went about twenty to ten.

Pause.

BARMAN: 'Evening News', was it?
MAN: Yes.

Pause.

Sometimes it's the 'Star' is the last to go.
BARMAN: Ah.
MAN: Or the . . . whatsisname.
BARMAN: 'Standard'.
MAN: Yes.

Pause.

All I had left tonight was the 'Evening News'.

Pause.

BARMAN: Then that went, did it?
MAN: Yes.

Pause.

Like a shot.

Pause.

BARMAN: You didn't have any left, eh?

MAN: No. Not after I sold that one.

Pause.

BARMAN: It was after that you must have come by here then, was it?

MAN: Yes, I come by here after that, see, after I packed up.

BARMAN: You didn't stop here though, did you?

MAN: When?

BARMAN: I mean, you didn't stop here and have a cup of tea then, did you?

MAN: What, about ten?

BARMAN: Yes.

MAN: No, I went up to Victoria.

BARMAN: No, I thought I didn't see you.

MAN: I had to go up to Victoria.

Pause.

BARMAN: Yes, trade was very brisk here about then.

Pause.

MAN: I went to see if I could get hold of George.

BARMAN: Who?

MAN: George.

Pause.

BARMAN: George who?

MAN: George . . . whatsisname.

BARMAN: Oh.

Pause.

Did you get hold of him?

MAN: No. No, I couldn't get hold of him. I couldn't locate him.

BARMAN: He's not about much now, is he?

Pause.

MAN: When did you last see him then?

BARMAN: Oh, I haven't seen him for years.

MAN: No, nor me.

Pause.

BARMAN: Used to suffer very bad from arthritis.
MAN: Arthritis?
BARMAN: Yes.
MAN: He never suffered from arthritis.
BARMAN: Suffered very bad.

Pause.

MAN: Not when I knew him.

Pause.

BARMAN: I think he must have left the area.

Pause.

MAN: Yes, it was the 'Evening News' was the last to go tonight.
BARMAN: Not always the last though, is it, though?
MAN: No. Oh no. I mean sometimes it's the 'News'. Other times it's one of the others. No way of telling beforehand. Until you've got your last one left, of course. Then you can tell which one it's going to be.
BARMAN: Yes.

Pause.

MAN: Oh yes.

Pause.

I think he must have left the area.

APPLICANT

An office. LAMB, *a young man, eager, cheerful, enthusiastic, is striding nervously, alone. The door opens.* MISS PIFFS *comes in. She is the essence of efficiency.*

PIFFS: Ah, good morning.
LAMB: Oh, good morning, miss.
PIFFS: Are you Mr. Lamb?
LAMB: That's right.
PIFFS [*studying a sheet of paper*]: Yes. You're applying for this vacant post, aren't you?
LAMB: I am actually, yes.
PIFFS: Are you a physicist?
LAMB: Oh yes, indeed. It's my whole life.
PIFFS [*languidly*]: Good. Now our procedure is, that before we discuss the applicant's qualifications we like to subject him to a little test to determine his psychological suitability. You've no objection?
LAMB: Oh, good heavens, no.
PIFFS: Jolly good.

MISS PIFFS has taken some objects out of a drawer and goes to LAMB. *She places a chair for him.*

PIFFS: Please sit down. [*He sits.*] Can I fit these to your palms?
LAMB [*affably*]: What are they?
PIFFS: Electrodes.
LAMB: Oh yes, of course. Funny little things.

She attaches them to his palms.

PIFFS: Now the earphones.

She attaches earphones to his head.

LAMB: I say how amusing.

PIFFS: Now I plug in.

She plugs in to the wall.

LAMB [*a trifle nervously*]: Plug in, do you? Oh yes, of course. Yes, you'd have to, wouldn't you?

MISS PIFFS *perches on a high stool and looks down on* LAMB.

This help to determine my . . . my suitability does it?

PIFFS: Unquestionably. Now relax. Just relax. Don't think about a thing.

LAMB: No.

PIFFS: Relax completely. Rela-a-a-x. Quite relaxed?

LAMB *nods.* MISS PIFFS *presses a button on the side of her stool. A piercing high pitched buzz-hum is heard.* LAMB *jolts rigid. His hands go to his earphones. He is propelled from the chair. He tries to crawl under the chair.* MISS PIFFS *watches, impassive. The noise stops.* LAMB *peeps out from under the chair, crawls out, stands, twitches, emits a short chuckle and collapses in the chair.*

PIFFS: Would you say you were an excitable person?

LAMB: Not—not unduly, no. Of course, I—

PIFFS: Would you say you were a moody person?

LAMB: Moody? No, I wouldn't say I was moody—well, sometimes occasionally I—

PIFFS: Do you ever get fits of depression?

LAMB: Well, I wouldn't call them depression exactly—

PIFFS: Do you often do things you regret in the morning?

LAMB: Regret? Things I regret? Well, it depends what you mean by often, really—I mean when you say often—

PIFFS: Are you often puzzled by women?

LAMB: Women?

PIFFS: Men.

LAMB: Men? Well, I was just going to answer the question about women—

PIFFS: Do you often feel puzzled?

LAMB: Puzzled?

PIFFS: By women.

LAMB: Women?

PIFFS: Men.

LAMB: Oh, now just a minute, I . . . Look, do you want separate answers or a joint answer?

PIFFS: After your day's work do you ever feel tired? Edgy? Fretty? Irritable? At a loose end? Morose? Frustrated? Morbid? Unable to concentrate? Unable to sleep? Unable to eat? Unable to remain seated? Unable to remain upright? Lustful? Indolent? On heat? Randy? Full of desire? Full of energy? Full of dread? Drained? of energy, of dread? of desire?

Pause.

LAMB [*thinking*]: Well, it's difficult to say really . . .

PIFFS: Are you a good mixer?

LAMB: Well, you've touched on quite an interesting point there—

PIFFS: Do you suffer from eczema, listlessness, or falling coat?

LAMB: Er . . .

PIFFS: Are you virgo intacta?

LAMB: I beg your pardon?

PIFFS: Are you virgo intacta?

LAMB: Oh, I say, that's rather embarrassing. I mean—in front of a lady—

PIFFS: Are you virgo intacta?

LAMB: Yes, I am, actually. I'll make no secret of it.

PIFFS: Have you always been virgo intacta?

LAMB: Oh yes, always. Always.

PIFFS: From the word go?

LAMB: Go? Oh yes, from the word go.

PIFFS: Do women frighten you?

She presses a button on the other side of her stool. The stage is plunged into redness, which flashes on and off in time with her questions.

PIFFS [*building*]: Their clothes? Their shoes? Their voices? Their laughter? Their stares? Their way of walking? Their way of sitting? Their way of smiling? Their way of talking? Their mouths? Their hands? Their feet? Their shins? Their thighs? Their knees? Their eyes?
Their [*Drumbeat*]. Their [*Drumbeat*]. Their [*Cymbal bang*]. Their [*Trombone chord*]. Their [*Bass note*].

LAMB [*in a high voice*]. Well it depends what you mean really—

The light still flashes. She presses the other button and the piercing buzz-hum is heard again. LAMB'S *hands go to his earphones. He is propelled from the chair, falls, rolls, crawls, totters and collapses.*

Silence.

He lies face upwards. MISS PIFFS *looks at him then walks to* LAMB *and bends over him.*

PIFFS: Thank you very much, Mr. Lamb. We'll let you know.